Triumphs of a *Little Girl*

A Memoir
Dr. Ingrid J. Benjamin Ph.D.

Copyright © 2021 by Dr. Ingrid J. Benjamin Ph.D.

All rights reserved. No part of this book may be reproduced in any form or by any electronic or mechanical means, including information storage and retrieval systems, without permission in writing from the publisher, except by reviewers, who may quote brief passages in a review.

This publication contains the opinions and ideas of its author. It is intended to provide helpful and informative material on the subjects addressed in the publication. The author and publisher specifically disclaim all responsibility for any liability, loss, or risk, personal or otherwise, which is incurred as a consequence, directly or indirectly, of the use and application of any of the contents of this book.

Scripture taken from the New King James Version ©. Copyright © 1982 by Thomas Nelson, Inc. Used by permission. All rights reserved.

WRITERS REPUBLIC L.L.C.
515 Summit Ave. Unit R1
Union City, NJ 07087, USA

Website: *www.writersrepublic.com*
Hotline: *1-877-656-6838*
Email: *info@writersrepublic.com*

Ordering Information:
Quantity sales. Special discounts are available on quantity purchases by corporations, associations, and others. For details, contact the publisher at the address above.

Library of Congress Control Number:	2021921049
ISBN-13: 978-1-63728-347-9	[Paperback Edition]
978-1-63728-348-6	[Digital Edition]

Rev. date: 10/05/2021

Acknowledgements

I thank God for gracing me with
the power to see this project through to the end.

I am thankful to God for placing Debra Starr along my pathway.
I thank and appreciate her for the support and encouragement
she has given me to get started on this journey.
Triumphs of a Little Girl came into fruition
because of her ingenuity in starting a memoir writing group.

I am grateful and appreciative to the Golden
Writers for tirelessly listening to my stories,
and for their valuable input and editing the contents of my articles.

I thank God for placing
Reverend Dr. Wilbert Jordan and Mrs. Deanna Jordan
along my pathway.
They have encouraged and tirelessly helped me to edit my book,
while sharing nuggets of wisdom with me.

I thank God for reuniting Dr. Marva Langhorne ThD,
my college batch mate with me. She has been a fresh
breath of inspiration and encouragement.
She helped to edit my story.

Dedication

To my grandmother, Mrs. Pearl Stewart,
who has raised me to become a phenomenal woman.

She has poured the recipes for life and living into my soul.

May God bless her soul.
Rest in Peace Mama!

Contents

Acknowledgements vii
Dedication viii
Introduction xi
A Child is Born 1
The Scourge of Infidelity 11
Move to New Amsterdam 19
The Awakening 26
Childhood Struggles for Education 32
My Grandmother and Me 62
Some Equipment in Mama's Home 79
My Cultural Heritage 86
The Day I Met My Father 112
Life Lessons I Learned From My Grandmother 119
Beginning Life After High School 135
The Death Of My Stepfather 160
My Grandparents 165
My Mentors 171
My Travels and Achievements Abroad 178
Reflections On My Childhood And God's Amazing Grace 184
My Second Act 197
Triumphs of a Little Girl Workbook 199

Introduction

As I sat down to pen my thoughts on my challenging childhood, I realized that this moment in my metamorphic transformation had prepared me for an unbelievable and even more challenging adulthood. I did not set this book in chronological order but in events, as I remember them.

This memoir chronicles my childhood as I transitioned into adulthood. It describes memories of my childhood, and my efforts to make it out of the ghetto. I did not place much emphasis on my life as an adult. I wanted the reader to see the result of my childhood preparation for what I thought would be a blissful adulthood. I got nothing free. I had to earn everything. There can be no greater reward than to achieve something you have worked very hard for.

My quest for success has taken me to worlds unknown. During my work and travels, I met the most amazing people. From the interiors and countryside of Guyana to Georgetown its capital, to the Caribbean, then to North America and the Middle East. It has been a life full of mountains, hills, valleys, and highways, but altogether a wonderful and rewarding one. One in which I celebrate with much gratitude to God and the many kind strangers whom I met along the way, who took the time to pause and gave me a helping hand.

My childhood dreams of imaginary places I have read about in books and living a successful life came through hard work and sacrifice. I hope that, as you read my book, you would see that my faith in God, tenacity, hard work, strategizing, focusing, and determination were some important keys to my success. I brought these principles forward into my adult life and found them to be valuable assets in my life journey. I always had a game plan. The takeaways are, "anything is possible if you try," and "never give up," as Mama always said in my darkest moments. I hope to encourage every youth struggling with the many pebbles or what may seem like gigantic rocks in your life, not to blame your circumstances but to accept responsibility for your own lives. Being bitter and angry with the people who might have made your life difficult only leads to discontentment, unhappiness, and self-destruction.

These events were not intended to be historical. Rather, it should be seen from the position of a seven to sixteen-year-old child, because that's the point of view in which this book is written. Only my opinions are adult in nature. I have changed the names of some protagonists to protect their identities.

Mama always advised me to take the higher road. Bitterness and revenge do not have a good payday. Instead, I always strived to strategize and plan for my future success. As a child, I realized that it was my life. What happened to my life depended on me. Even at a tender age, I realized that I was responsible for how my life turned out. Therefore, I had to prepare myself for what I wanted my life to be. I do not believe in "faking it till you make it," because in faking it, I will always have to work to impress others, who may have unrealistic expectations of me. I believe in being authentic to myself and everyone, and doing the best I can with what I have. Like Mama always told me, "put your best foot forward." Good luck and may you find the peace and passion for life that only comes from a Higher Power as you traverse this challenging world.

A Child is Born

A child's birth, in many circumstances, is embraced with happiness, love and anticipation for a bright future. Mine was different...

Nestled in the northeast edge of the South American Plate lies a little country named Guyana, formerly known as British Guiana. We are fortunate to have neighbors such as Suriname, Brazil and Venezuela. Guyana is the only English-speaking country in this part of the world, which is South America. A beautiful country, known for its lush green rainforests and mountain ranges, rich soil and minerals, gold and diamonds, cascading waterfalls, large rivers, black and clear waters, a melting pot of peoples of many races, religions, and cultures and now an oil-rich Mecca. It's a blessed and beautiful country. I am proud to have been born in this magnificent country.

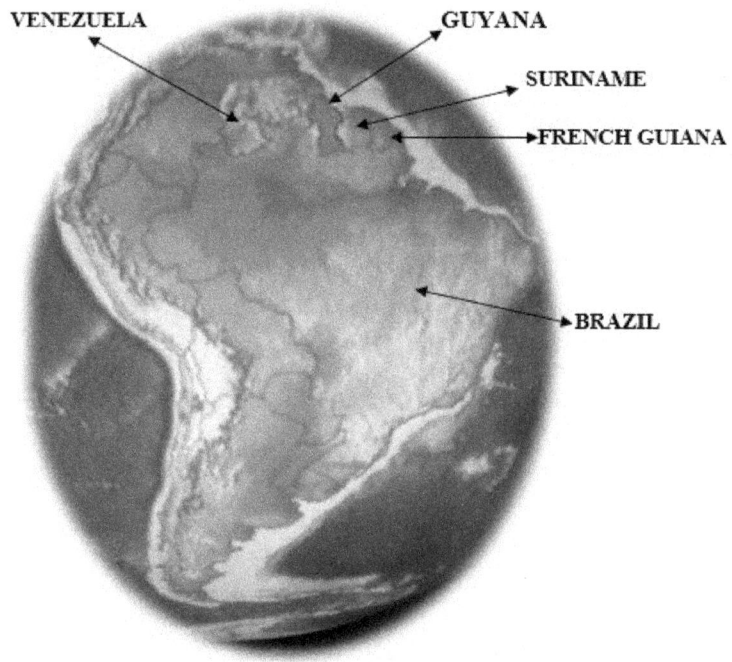

Map of South America Showing the Position of Guyana and its Neighbors

This is my story. As I sit down to pen my story, I feel a sense of loss and deep sadness as tears flow profusely down my cheeks. I stopped for a while and thought I could not continue. It felt as though I was reliving the abuses of my childhood and many parts of my adulthood. After a few days, I got an epiphany, an "aha" moment. I realized that I did nothing wrong. I was only a child. This circumstance should not hold me captive or responsible for the dysfunction that the adults in my life created around me. I did not cry when I was a child! Why should I cry now? Maybe someone, somewhere, may learn from my experiences and bold resolve to get ahead in this world.

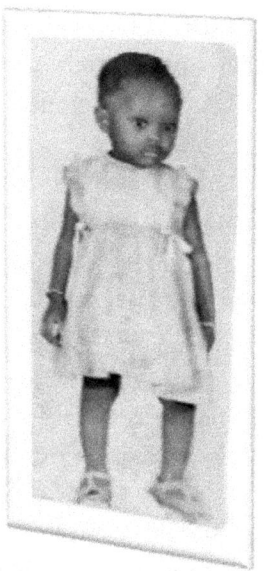

My picture - Mama gave me the gold bracelets I am wearing.

It began when a baby girl was born to two young unwed parents. She was named Ingrid Juliana. The birth of a child usually brings happiness and a sense of joy and pride and anticipation to prepare this child to have a happy, successful future. This was not my reality. There were five negative factors related to my birth:

- Being born out of wedlock at that time in history was considered an embarrassment to the family. When many young ladies became pregnant, they suddenly vanished. They were sent to live with relatives far away until they gave birth. Then they emerged from seclusion without the babies. The babies were either given to other relatives to raise or would join the family later for the maternal grandmother to raise as her own or adopted child. I wondered what the point of this secrecy was. When you live in a small community, everyone knew everybody's business, anyway.

This was not the case with me. My mother had nowhere to hide. My father got two women pregnant at the same time. He already had a child with another woman who was now carrying his second child. He later married her.

- Opportunities were slim or nonexistent for the poor. I was a bastard child living in a British colony with British Laws. A wonderful existence meant that you had to not only keep up with the status quo but be a part of it. We had none of it.

- Next, my father left my mother before I was born. This meant that it fractured the usual and acceptable family structure for me.

- I was born dark-skinned and poor to a mother who had very little education and she was a maid, also called a domestic servant. This meant that she could not adequately take care of me, while providing the basic necessities of life for herself. The structure of the economic system favored the rich at this time.

- These were not attributes for a successful life, according to societal norms at that time. Sure enough, they expected me to follow in the footsteps of my mother or fall through the cracks beneath her into a life of degradation. As a child, I found myself living and moving often between my mother, aunt, and grandmother, until my grandmother took me, thus bringing some amount of permanency and stability to my young life.

Map of Guyana showing my travels for Work & Study as well as our neighbors – Suriname, Brazil and Venezuela

I was born in New Amsterdam, then I moved to Linden (also called McKenzie). I moved back and forth (between New Amsterdam and Linden) a few times by the time I was eight years old. I lived with my mother, aunt, mother again, and then, finally, with my grandmother.

After high School, I went to my mother in Linden in search of a secretarial position in the bauxite industry. Later, I traveled from Linden to the Capital, Georgetown, to the Catholic Diocese searching for a teaching position. My assignment was an assistant teacher on the Pakaraima Mountains in the Interior.

Later I went to work with Minister Duncan as his confidential secretary in the Ministry of Regional Development in another part of the Interior - Lethem. I travelled throughout the Rupununi Savannah. The terrain in Lethem is characterized as Flatlands. In the distance, I could see the majestic Kanuku Mountain Range.

After leaving the Interior, I went back to New Amsterdam to work in the Regional Development Office as a typist. College was calling, so I left and entered Lilian Dewar College of Education in Georgetown to study Science. After college, I went to work in Linden and New Amsterdam Multilateral Schools.

Three years after my unceremonious entry into this world, my mother gave birth to my sister, still out of wedlock. However, she was light-skinned and thus having a "shoe in" for acceptance. Then, my mother and my sister's father separated. The cycle continued with a third child, another girl, Carol, from someone else. She was dark-skinned and shared the same fate as me. Being of kindred spirits, we became best friends even to this day. Later, my mother made up with her second child's father. She got pregnant again, and this time, they got married. My mother had nine children in wedlock. She barely recognized her two bastard children (Carol and me), whom she treated with utter disdain. I think it embarrassed her to know we were her children.

Carol and Me

At one point, she expressed that she wanted all of her children to live together. In retrospect, I do not see the importance or significance of this master plan. She often referred to my other siblings as "her children" and would say to me harshly, "You do not like my children." This was mindboggling to me since I was only a child, and I dare not touch "her children" otherwise, I would have been beaten. Carol and I stayed away from them because we considered them to be elite and better than us. My sister and I were fed last at every meal from what were left over at the bottom of the pot. Since I was dark-skinned, I had to do the dishes, and the pots were left for my special touch. My siblings did not do any chores in the home. My "mother's children" slept on beds while my sister, Carol, and I slept on the floors on rags called bedding. Even when my sister and I lived with my grandmother and my siblings came to visit on vacations, we had to give up our beds and sleep on the floor. As children, we had no toys when we lived with our mother and we could not play with "my mother's children's" toys. However, when they came to visit us, they played with our toys and destroyed all of them before they left. This was a horrifying experience since we only received toys once a year at Christmas, and not more than two. We tried to keep our toys from one year to the next, so we had an accumulation of toys to play with all year round.

They blamed us for everything that went wrong in this dysfunctional household. For example, one day, some neighborhood kids were playing "flip" under the front stairs of our house. Burt fell and screamed. All the other kids ran away. I remained there and tried to help him to get back on his feet to walk home. When he could not stand, I ran to get his mother, who came and lifted him home. Later, we learned that his foot was broken. I cannot remember which foot. My mother blamed me for breaking Burt's foot. I was only about seven years old when this incident occurred. My mother held this "over my head" for the next eleven years. Finally, I asked her to stop. I told her that it was an accident and that everyone ran away. I was the only one who stayed to help Burt. This made matters worse. She said that I was rude to her. I left it alone because I realized that I just could not win because she never believed me.

Another incident that occurred was when my mother came to visit with my siblings. Some money was missing. Almost immediately, the blame was directed towards Carol. Meanwhile, all the other children in the house knew who took the money. We kept looking at an older brother anticipating that he would own up to it and come clean. He just stood there and watched while Carol was falsely accused. Up to this point, I had never seen so much anger and rage as when our mother was hitting Carol. She hit her with open hands and a fist while calling her a thief. Carol was crying and pleading her innocence. Then, suddenly, I saw my mother ripped off her clothes, exposing her breasts and underwear. She was now naked. She screamed even harder. She caught pieces of her dress and tried to cover herself. She was still exposed for everyone to see. The money was not found, and our mother was still enraged. I got out of there with lightning speed because I knew I would be the next victim. I went to my usual hiding place in the cemetery. When I emerged hours later, Carol had recovered and was sitting downstairs in the chicken coup with her chickens, a familiar place for her.

They never found the money. Honesty did not prevail that day, and they blamed Carol for the next week and a half, which was the end of my mother's visit. She never repaired Carol's dress or made a new one for her, even though she made dresses for her other children. Carol only had the bare necessities of clothing to begin with. I had to give her one of mine. Anyway, she wore most of my clothing when I grew out of them. "Hand-me-downs" or old clothes as they were called. What a human travesty! My mother made a clear distinction between her children, those whom she loved and cherished, because she was married to their father. Then there were the unworthy and unloved ones such as Carol and me.

Meanwhile, my stepfather was rarely at home. He was at work or out with his friends or mistresses. Whenever he was at home, he would play with all of us or pass the time away fighting with my mother. As a child, I never understood the reason for such fights. They were often loud and physically abusive. After each fight, he got dressed and left home. He returned late at night and sometimes to resume where he left off.

Living in this unstable environment, in a dysfunctional family, only fostered a sense of fear and uncertainty in my young life. Many times, I would retreat in a corner with my sister. We were voiceless, and we felt we did not belong here or anywhere as a matter of fact. Our fathers were not an integral part of our lives. We never saw or knew who they were. They neither visited nor supported us. I later learned that my mother took my father to court to force him to support me, while Carol's father migrated to England. To this day, I do not know my father. And to add insult to injury, I am carrying his last name. My grandmother told me that if I used his name, it would help me know him. To my mind, this idea was wishful thinking and futile because I still don't know him, and I am way past my fortieth birthday. My sister suffered more than me. But, it's her story to tell. I only hope that she will find the strength and wisdom to do so, to bring about the much-needed closure that she deserves.

As a child, I had serious issues with God. Where was He when I needed him the most? Why didn't He help me? I found it hard to believe when I was told that "God loves me." Why would He love someone like me? I asked myself. I was brought up in the church, where they speak about love and happiness. However, my realities were quite the opposite. This creates conflicts in a child's mind. My inferiority complex was at an all-time low. I kept asking myself, "Why was I born dark-skinned?" This question originated because I was often described as black in the most derogatory manner and tone. They made me feel as though I was less than my siblings or other light-skinned children. When my younger sister (who was fair-skinned) and I were out in public, the adults would gravitate towards her and say how pretty she was, and they would even give her money. When they were finished talking with her, they turned and walked away. They left me standing there as though I were invisible. "Why wasn't I born beautiful?" They often referred to me as black and ugly. Most people are proud of their hair. As a child, I heard that "the hair is a woman's beauty." I was told that my hair was hard and nappy. As compared to my siblings' hair that was "nice and soft." No child should ever feel this way.

Dr. Ingrid J. Benjamin Ph.D.

My Grandmother - Mama and Me

The Scourge of Infidelity

When adults become selfish and egotistical,
the effects of this behavior on children are often forgotten or ignored.
Many children may suffer in silence as they develop
defensive techniques that may lead to maladaptive behaviors.
I was blessed to have a grandmother who cared.

A very confusing incident occurred when I was a child, one that has left me with lingering questions. I was about seven years old, when my mother relocated with my two sisters, brother and me to live in another house. When we arrived, a tall fair skinned gentleman greeted us and helped us with our luggage. I was told to go inside. As I entered the house, I noticed the back door was opened. Being curious, I walk through the house towards the back door and I noticed a woman and a child walking away. They were both looking over their shoulders towards me. It was a male child approximately three years old and he was crying out, "daddy, daddy, daddy." The woman gripped his tiny hand firmly in an effort to prevent him from escaping. I stood there transfixed, as they vanished from sight.

Meanwhile, my mother and the gentleman were putting our luggage away. She gave us a snack. The gentleman was playing with my brother and one of my sisters, who addressed him as "Daddy," so I joined in the fun and also addressed him as "daddy" too. However, my mother rebuked me harshly saying, "That's not your father, he is Uncle Freddie."

A few days later, my mother enrolled me in Mackenzie primary school. I must have been placed in standard one. She took me to school in the morning, but did not return for me during the lunch break. All of the children left to go to their several homes, while I stood there wondering how to find my home. I set out in the direction where I thought my house was located but nothing seemed familiar. I began to cry. I was afraid. A young lady appeared clad in a white dress with pretty blue flowers and asked why I was crying. I explained that I wanted to go home but I could not find my house. She asked where I lived, and I replied that I don't know. She took me back to school, where we met one of the teachers who recognized me as a new student. She gave my address to the young lady who accompanied me to my new home. I related the incident to my mother, she gave me my lunch and decided that she was not going to take me to school until the following day. The next few days flew by quickly as I got adjusted to my new neighborhood and school.

One afternoon, on my way home alone, I stopped by Ms. Marie's house to buy a fruity (frozen fruit flavored icicle). I began to walk home slowly, while enjoying my fruity. Suddenly, I felt a thump on the back of my head, my fruity went flying into the middle of the street. Another thump followed in quick succession, on my head, then my school bag went flying in another direction. A third thump caught me on my shoulder which caused me to fall, hitting my head. I scream. When I was able to get up, I saw an older student and another young lady walking away and laughing. I picked up my bag, and cried all the way home. When I arrived home, my mother inquired what has happened, I related the incident to her. She remained silent and continued doing her work. I proceeded to the bathroom and took a shower. That night, my head and shoulders hurt so badly I could hardly sleep. When I awoke in the morning a lump had grown on my forehead. Uncle Freddie saw the lump and asked what happened. Before I could answer, my younger sister shouted, "she got beat up" and began laughing. I was in so much pain, I returned to bed.

Later that day, when I heard my grandmother's voice, I ran outside and grabbed on to her. She held me and asked what happened. I related the whole story to her. She made an ice pack and put it on my forehead. She put me on her lap and massaged my neck and shoulders with coconut oil. I must have fallen asleep, because Mama as I fondly called her, was shaking me lightly and telling me to have some tea. I stayed on Mama's lap and drank the tea while eating bread and peanut butter. Lunchtime met me in the same position. A few hours later, when Mama was ready to go, she asked me to get up. I latched on to her and buried my head in her breast and would not let her go. Then she promised to return the next weekend. I let go very slowly but reluctantly. You see, Mama worked in Watooka as a maid and was only given one day off a week, on Saturday or Sunday. She could have chosen which day she preferred. She could only visit us on her day off.

The following day I saw the young ladies next door at our neighbor's house. The one who abused me, licked her tongue out and fanned her dress at me. I went inside and told my mother. She came out to see who the person was. When she saw them, she said that was the neighbor's cousins. The one who abused me was Dede who was more than twice my age.

As usual, Monday morning came and I had to go to school. In the afternoon after school, I saw Dede waiting for me at the corner of the street I passed on my way home. I took another route home thus avoiding another encounter. The following day, after school I looked around, but I did not see her. I thought all was clear, so I went to buy my fruity, and proceeded on my way home. 'Whack' I felt a blow on my back. My fruity and my bag fell out of my hands. Dede proceeded to hit me on my chest and arms. Even though I was screaming and crying, she did not stop until she was satisfied. People passed by and looked and no one stopped her or helped me.

This bullying continued, almost on a daily basis. My mother and stepfather said nothing and did nothing about it. After a while, my mother stopped asking what happened. I was beaten to a pulp, and always in pain but no one helped me. School in the afternoons had become a place of 'gloom and doom' for me. Many times, I sat at the bottom of the back stairs after lunch and cried because I did not want to go back to school. My mother always looked out of the back door and yelled at me to go to school. Whenever Mama came to visit on the weekend and saw my frail, bruised, scratched and battered body, she asked what happened and got the same story all over again. She asked my mother harshly one day, "Leda, why you allow these people to beat up this pickney?" My mother said, "Ingrid has to fight for herself." Mama was massaging my body with coconut oil. She stopped immediately, put me to lie on the sofa and went next door. I do not know what was said. But Mama came back, picked me up and continued to massage my body.

Monday came as usual. I went to school. In the afternoon I was preparing for my usual beat down. I was relieved, I did not see Dede.

As a matter of fact, I did not see her for the entire week. My seven-year-old body got a break from battering. I believe, if this had continued, I would have died. I was battered to the point where I could hardly eat or write in school. It must have been several weeks later; I was recovering very well. I was able to do my school work and eat a whole meal, when I saw Dede again. She was approaching me. This time I was ready. When she came close to me, I wacked her in the face with my school bag and ran away as fast as I could. I didn't even look back. She never approached me again, nor said anything to me. Every time I saw her, I was ready. I took a stance and waited for her. Even when I saw her in the yard while I was playing, I stopped and got ready for her. I told myself, if I couldn't hit her with something, then I was going to bite her as hard as I could. I had some sharp teeth and they were going to be put to good use. She probably read my mind, she never bothered me again.

I never understood why I was getting beaten, when I did nothing wrong. I did not know anyone in my neighborhood. When some of the younger children saw my sister and I playing in the yard, they came over and played with us. But whenever their mothers saw them, they were called away and sometimes spanked. It appeared as though we were the outcasts. No one talked with my mother either. I noticed whenever she said good morning to the neighbors, they turned their heads and did not respond. Some of them hissed their teeth and gave her the ugly eyes while turning their heads away. I did not have that problem, after the first unresponsive "good morning," from every adult, I never hailed anyone else again. I felt that they did not like me.

Several months, elapsed. I was beginning to get accustomed to living in this weird neighborhood. My grandmother showed up for what I thought would be her regular visit. This time she brought several bags, and a bicycle. She announced to my mother that she was done with working in Watooka and was going back to New Amsterdam to live, and that she was taking me to live with her. Here I was again, making another move. By this time, I had moved several times between my mother and aunt and now my grandmother was taking me. A few weeks before, my aunt came and took my youngest sister at that time, Carol to live with her father's mother on the West Coast of Berbice. My mother continued to live with my two siblings and her husband in the same neighborhood.

As the years went by, my mother often came to our home on vacation, or to give birth to her children. During these times the main topic of discussion usually centered around Uncle Freddie's mistresses, and how abusive he was, the neighbors, and how unhappy she was. However, at the end of her vacations, she always returned. There was also talk about witchcraft and paranormal activities in her home. My mother said her husband's mistresses sent spirits to harm her. For instance, when my younger sister was about ten years old, she saw snakes in her school bag. No one else saw those snakes. As a result, she did not want to go to school. She was eventually sent to live with us. Mama bought her a new bag, those snakes disappeared and she was able to attend school.

You may be wondering what is going on in this story? It was very real and complicated.

As a child, I was always listening, but could not join in the conversation because I was often told that children should be seen and not heard. So being inquisitive, I paid attention and began to put the pieces of this puzzle together. What I learned was mind boggling. Ok, let's go back to the beginning of my story. Remember the woman and little boy I saw walking and looking back? Her name was Maxine, the little boy's name was Cedric. She was my stepfather's mistress. She and Cedric were living with Uncle Freddie for many years. He met her with Cedric when he was a new born. Even though Cedric was not his biological child, he raised him as his own, but did not legally adapt him. He proposed to my mother, after she became pregnant with his third child and while he was still living with Maxine. I do not know the circumstances in which Maxine was informed about Uncle Freddie's impending nuptial; but I know that I did not attend the wedding or reception. I learned that my mother and Uncle Freddie were married quietly by a judge. Maxine refused to leave regardless.

Never the less, she left hurriedly when she saw my mother began moving in. Hence, he had one woman moving in, while the other one moving out at the same time. This was the reason for the back door being opened.

Now for the neighbors! Some of them were related to Maxine while the others were her friends and drinking buddies. So, when she was forced out, her departure caused this tight bond to be broken. This made the neighbors furious, and they directed all of their anger towards us. On the other hand, I do not understand why I was constantly attacked by Dede. I can only assume that she felt it was her duty to represent her cousin, or that after she beat me up, we would leave and her cousins would return. This animosity towards my mother and siblings continued for several years after my departure from Mackenzie. Meanwhile, my stepfather continued to sleep with Maxine, and supported Cedric who also took his last name. Whenever Maxine met my mother in the street, she always taunted her and let her know that she's got her man and would not leave him.

My stepfather continued his philandering. Having two families were not enough for him. He got himself a third family. So, while my mother was having his babies, he was also having babies with someone else. This second woman Darlene used to taunt my mother whenever she saw her. His third family came to light after his death.

Once again, I have reason to question the condition of the human heart. Even as a child I wondered why my mother kept going back for more punishment. She was unhappy at home, in the neighborhood and whenever she was out shopping, she always encountered one of her husband's mistresses. Moreover, she had no friends. She did nothing outside the home for fun. She had a younger brother who seldom visited, and she did not want him to get involved in her business. As an adult I realized that my mother was raised in a dysfunctional household and that is all she knew. Even though her father never spanked her or any of her siblings, she witnessed him abusing Mama, (her mother) consistently. Maybe she thought this was normal, since her mother endured similar forms of abuse. I don't know. After several years, she left her husband and went home to her mother with the younger children.

I am unable to ask my mother the burning questions on my mind because I believe she will tell me to mind my business, I was being rude. A few of the questions I would like to ask her were: "Why didn't you help me when I was getting beaten." "Did you know Uncle Freddie was a player when you met him?" "Did you know he was living with someone when he proposed to you? "Why did you stay with him so long, even though you were being abused?" Somehow, I felt my mother had prior knowledge of her husband's living situation before they were married, because she recognized Dede by name and as the neighbor's cousin. This is not knowledge that could be obtained accidentally. This adds more questions to the "soap opera". "What were accomplished in these scenarios?" Did anyone feel satisfied with their behavior? I am lost for words on this one so, I will leave it alone. I realize that I may never find answers to my questions nor understand why civility and respect does not always prevail in humanity.

Move to New Amsterdam

When adults make decisions, good or bad, children are caught in the crosshairs. The circumstances that follow may be difficult and confusing for the children. The outcome can have serious and unintended consequences, not to mention mind-boggling for the children. For me, this move meant stability and preparation for adulthood.

I was living with my mother in McKenzie (now called Linden), a place where bauxite and alumina were mined, when one day my grandmother showed up unannounced with her baggage and told my mother that she was going back to New Amsterdam to live and that she would take "Buggy" (that's me) with her. My grandmother worked as a domestic servant (maid) for several years in Watooka. (Expatriates and qualified Guyanese who were supervisors, worked in the same mining area lived here.) She left my grandfather after enduring years of physical and emotional abuse. He had passed away by this time. I was about eight years old when my grandmother came to get me. My mother had no reaction to this proposal. She did not even protest or show any signs of disapproval that she was losing her oldest child. I am not sure, but I think my grandmother demanded to take me instead of making a request. She could be very authoritative when she wanted. That night, my mother packed my few pieces of clothes (my "Georgie bundle" as it was called) in an old "grip" (suitcase.)

The next morning, we started on our journey. We traveled all day long. First, on a boat called the "RH Carr." This was a motor vessel (ferry) that ran between McKenzie and Georgetown along the Demerara River. It carried passengers and a small amount of cargo. It took several hours to get to its destination.

The next leg of the trip was by train. The train ran between Georgetown and Rosignol. This was the fun part. As the train stopped at different villages along the way, there were food and fruits on sale. I had an enjoyable time as I "chowed down" on everything I could eat. We traveled for several hours.

When we got to Rosignol, we took another ferry called the Torani, which ran between Rosignol and New Amsterdam along the Berbice River. This part of the trip took about an hour because the boat was going in an oblique direction across the Berbice River. It was often late, or it broke down and had to be repaired. When this happened, passengers waiting on the stelling (wharf) had to go to Blairmont to take a smaller boat called a launch. The last leg of this trip was by taxi, sometimes called a hired car or by bus. May God help you if you were stuck on the Torani when it broke down. Sometimes it was pulled along the river by barges. We were finally home that night. I was sick and tired, perhaps from eating too much on the train. I went straight to bed without unpacking or saying my prayers.

Mama awakened me early the next morning. She wanted me to have a shower and get dressed to go to school. I jumped out of bed and ran into the kitchen to see my new home and its surroundings. I stood on the inside of our wooden back door which was in two parts–top and bottom. I opened the top half while the bottom was closed. I saw an enormous yard with four tiny houses side by side in front and a duplex at the back. It appeared that one family occupied each house. The children were carrying buckets of water into their houses. I guess they were preparing to go to school, too. There was one bathroom, two out-houses or latrines, connected side by side, and one standpipe for everyone in the yard to use. There was no running water in the houses except for one. This would be my residence for the next ten years.

The Stand Pipe
This was our primary source of water supply. We filled our buckets and took them into the house for cleaning, drinking, and doing the laundry. We also took the water into the only community bathroom for showers. As children, we took baths under the standpipe with our clothes on – Some of us.

Somehow this environment seemed familiar to me. I had lived here with my aunt prior to living with my mother. I cannot remember all the circumstances that preceded my movement between my mother and my aunt. However, as a child, the adults made the decisions, and I just had to move with the flow. My aunt continued to live with us or we were living with her. I do not know the complete story. What I knew was that my grandmother paid for the rent.

I told my grandmother whom I called Mama (I was told that I gave her that name when I started to talk. I also renamed my aunt, uncles, and grandfather.), that I wanted to go to the bathroom. She presented me with a white, round, medium-sized pot with painted red and yellow flowers and green leaves all around it. The top edge was curved outwards, I suppose for comfort. I later found out that there were many names for it, including Potty, Po, Posey, and Commode.

A Potty
Used in the house as a toilet, especially during the nights. In the mornings and evenings, we threw it out into the latrine, then we cleaned and sanitized it with Jaye's Fluid.

I had breakfast then placed my plate and cup in a wooden sink called a trough which projected outwards from the kitchen window. I picked up a bucket, filling it with water from the only standpipe in the yard. Mama gave me a half calabash to pour water on my body while I had a shower in the community bathroom. She also gave me soap and a towel to take into the bathroom. When I was finished bathing, I went back into the house. I got dressed and my grandmother took me to a church school–Mission Chapel Congregational. They placed me in Standard Two. This was a public school, even though it was named after the church.

The education system in Guyana differed from the United States. Standard Two is equivalent to Grade 2. A student could remain here in elementary school until they leave, either for high school at age ten to twelve or until they leave school altogether, between sixteen and eighteen years old. They had a choice to go to Commercial (business school) or Trade school or even seek employment when they leave. A small percentage of students would stick around to write the national exams, which would equip them for higher education. These examinations were the "Preliminary Certificate Examination" (PC) and the "College of Preceptors Examination" (CP). There were no graduation ceremonies. Students left at their own choosing. The grading system differed from the U.S.A. There were no alphabetical grades. Instead, students were graded and ranked as a percentage or given a numerical grade for each course or subject. The first three highest overall averages were recognized, and they gave the students awards in the form of certificates during the school assembly at the end of each semester. There were three semesters in each school year. Parents and guardians purchased all textbooks and school supplies for their children.

School started promptly at 8:30 in the morning with prayers and the reciting of Bible verses and ended at 11:30 for lunch. Lunch was 1 ½ hour long. The afternoon session began at 1:00 and ended at 3:00. The students and teachers lived in the community, so everyone went home for lunch. Mama bought some material and gave it to a dressmaker (also called a seamstress) to make my school uniform. The little girls wore white blouses under a navy dress like a uniform with pleated skirts attached, while some of the older girls wore white shirts and pleated navy skirts. The others wore the whole uniform. It was their choice. My uniform was an excellent fit, and I could blend in with the other little girls in my school. The young men wore white shirts and long khaki pants, while the boys wore white shirts and short khaki pants. The footwear was optional. Students, both male and female, wore whatever shoes their parents could afford. Some students wore socks and shoes, some wore shoes without socks, and others wore sneakers or yachting shoes with or without socks, and others wore slippers. The color of our uniforms identified students and the schools they attended. Each school had a different color uniform. For example, the girls in St. Theresa's Catholic School wore brown uniforms with cream blouses while the boys wore brown pants and cream shirts.

Mission Chapel School
The old school as it stands today – renovated and different.
We used to play in the courtyard.
There were no windows. The roof was extended.
When it rained, we did not get wet. There were no individual classrooms.

Mission Chapel Church

Students attended the church on special occasions such as Easter and Christmas.

Some of our assemblies and concerts were also held in the church.

The Awakening

Childhood friendships are like treasured oysters. They may seem insignificant on the outside but on the inside are the tasty goodness of love and innocent affection that makes them special, desirable, and memorable! Some adults have amnesia and forget how precious their own childhood friendships were.

I was awakened to the fact that adults send mixed messages which may cause children to become conflicted and less likely to express themselves truthfully.

I had a friend named Sharon, who lived in a sizeable house obliquely across the street. She was Sister Ray's granddaughter. Every day after school, we walked home together while chatting about school or just about any random thing that caught the attention of two eight to nine-year-old children. I noticed that as soon as we turned the corner of our street, she started walking faster and I had to run to catch up with her, and she left me without saying goodbye. One afternoon, Sharon's older brother Robby saw us walking together. He said to her, in a very harsh tone, "Why are you talking to her? Didn't you hear granny say, you must not speak to her?" Sharon looked at me so sadly as if to say, "I'm sorry." She bent her head in embarrassment and walked away.

We never spoke again. Even though this was one of my many open rejections, it was a surprise to me. I went home feeling very sad and confused because Sister Ray was my Sunday school teacher. She always talked to me nicely and gave the children snacks after Sunday school. I told Mama what happened when she came home that evening. She hissed her teeth and said, "Sister Ray is too damn deceitful." I then told her I did not want to go back to her Sunday school. Mama said to me, "You have something to do for the Christmas concert, go back and show them what you can do." Christmas came a few weeks later. Mama bought me a new outfit, hair ribbons, dress, socks, and shoes. I went to the concert. When my name was called, I stood up and went in front of the class and proudly recited my poem as a professional artiste. The little gathering of students, parents, and friends went wild. They stood up and clapped for me and called for an encore. I went back on stage and performed better. At this point, I knew that I was a "showoff." Everyone wanted more. Mama shouted, "That's my grandchild." When it was over, everyone came over and congratulated me. That was my last attendance at this Sunday school.

After several weeks of my noticeable absence, Sister Ray asked Mama why I could not go back to Sunday school. In a harsh tone, Mama said, "You are a damn hypocrite," and she walked away. I guess it's hard to explain to a child the gray areas of this life when it comes to friendship and the many hurdles one has to go through to achieve success in maintaining such friendships—especially while facing the harsh realities of poverty and non-acceptance.

In retrospect, I believe that Sister Ray, like many others, did not want their children and grandchildren to associate with someone who lived in a tenement yard where there were fighting, cursing, stealing, gambling, loud music, and many lewd behaviors daily. The exposure to such behaviors can have a negative effect on children. I now understand why I could not always go outside to play with the other children in the yard, especially during cursing and fighting episodes. Mama was not at home during the day. After school in the afternoons, I was usually at home alone. Staying in the house was my domain and sanctuary. I played with my toys and used the chairs as my imaginary friends, who were also my "students." I read to myself and "friends" every day after school. Later, my grandmother took me to work and everywhere she went. She often said to me, "I don't want you to associate with certain elements." Or she said, "Show me your company and I'll tell you who you are." By the phrase "certain elements," she meant people with a questionable or negative reputation. My second sister, Carol, later joined us; I now had someone to play with, or so I thought!

Carol was about three-to-four years old when she came to live with us. I am five years older than her. She was silent and stayed in a corner all day long. Whenever I tried to play with her, she did not respond. I thought perhaps that she did not like me. I kept trying to talk and play with her, anyway. She lived with her paternal grandmother in a little village on the west coast of Berbice. By now, you know that we did not have the same father. My mother instructed my aunt to take Carol and give her to a teacher who lived in our town. I do not know the full details of this transaction. But, when my aunt came home with Carol, she said to Mama, "You do not give your children away to strangers." So, Carol stayed with us and ultimately became my aunt's responsibility, one which she never took seriously. It seemed as though my aunt just did not care sometimes. My aunt never took an interest in Carol's wellbeing. Carol ate, slept and used the bathroom in that corner. She never attempted to move from that spot. Our aunt never fed her, or changed her, or played with her. She never took care of Carol. I fed her and took care of her. Whenever Mama came home and found that Carol messed in her underwear, she spanked her.

After a while, I changed and cleaned her up before Mama came home and showed her how to use the potty. I just could not see her being spanked. It scared me, and it made me sad. I even cleaned her up, taught her to say her prayers and took her to bed at night. Mama never spanked me. She rolled her eyes and looked at me harshly with a disapproving stare whenever something was out of order, or I was getting "beside myself," as she often said. That sent a message to me, that was, "Don't mess with Mama!" After what seemed like several weeks, Carol socialized with me. We played together in her corner and she began to talk, and she moved around the house freely, but as if walking on eggshells. We were often left alone at home while Mama and our aunt went to work. Carol and I became friends, and we did everything together.

Even though I was a child, I knew that Carol's treatment was wrong, but, for some unknown reason, I could not express it. I could only render help as much as an eight to nine-year-old could. As I reflect on this and other incidents that occurred, I realize that this was painful and did not fit the norms of what should have been a psychosocially balanced childhood. No child should have to experience such atrocities. This presented another moral dilemma. Even at the age of three, no one saw that Carol was not used to interacting with anyone because of her odd behavior. This reflected on what happened in her previous home. Next, our aunt took care of other people's children but not Carol. However, this is Carol's story to tell. I hope that she will give herself permission to speak her truth into existence because despite everything, she has done well for herself. I am very proud of her. I know that someone somewhere may benefit because of her own revelations of childhood struggles and how she overcame them.

Moving forward a few years, I had another friend, Ann Marie. We were the same age, fourteen-years-old. We went to the same elementary school, and we were in the same classes. Sometimes we visited each other on the weekends. We went to Mrs. Delaney, our needlecraft teacher's home, on some weekends to help her make cakes whenever she had an event, this friendship was welcomed. Mama knew Ann Marie's parents and she approved of them because they were outstanding citizens in the community. All my friendships had to be preapproved by Mama. This friendship was soon dissolved. Ann Marie went to visit her pen-pal in

McKenzie. She became pregnant. She dropped out of school. I continued to visit her on some weekends. I did not tell Mama anything for fear that she would break up our friendship. Somehow, she found out. She came home one evening "in a huff and a puff" and told me not to speak with Ann Marie anymore. Immediately, I knew that she found out Ann Marie was pregnant, so I did not ask why.

This was the typical dynamics of a small town. The news went around quickly, and everybody got entangled into everybody's business, whether it concerned them or not. News of pregnancy went around like wildfire. That became the town's gossip. By the time I heard of it again, "Ann Marie was pregnant by her father." No one knew who the baby's father was. He did not live in the town. Wahoo!

From a child's point of view, these incidents could be mindboggling. On one hand, there was Sister Ray, who did not want her grandchild to be my friend because of my social and economic stature in life. I lived in the ghetto. On the other hand, my grandmother did not want me to be Ann Marie's friend because it created a similar moral and social dilemma. Sister Ray thought I would be a negative influence on Sharon, while Mama thought that Ann Marie would negatively influence me. While these situations could become a reality, the adults, in their good intentions, did not seek to explain their respective expectations for us. We were just given orders to follow, as soldiers on the battlefield.

When I think about this situation, Mama was accusing Sister Ray of the same things that she herself was doing. In my mind, this was also hypercritical, especially coming from someone like my grandmother, who had been at the receiving end of negativity herself. I will discuss this later. After a while, I could not play with the children in the yard. The phrase "certain elements" comes to mind again. Mama thought that they were not good enough to play with me.

The infamous pencil case illustrates another incident of adult's deceit and unfairness. One evening, just after dinner, we heard a loud knocking on our front door. I opened the door to find Patrice's mom standing outside. In a loud tone, she said, "I want Patrice's pencil case; you stole it from her in school today." Trembling, I said, "I did not steal her pencil case." When I looked in the dark, Patrice was hiding behind her mother. Her mom insisted that I stole her pencil case. My mother came to the door to see who was creating a ruckus. When the two ladies saw each other, there was instant silence. They were friends who had not seen each other for several years. After a brief silence, they began talking. My mother told me to give up my pencil case. My grandmother said, "No, Ingrid bought this pencil case a few days ago." My mother kept saying that I must return the pencil case to Patrice and tried to take it away from me. I held on to my case and did not let it go. Mama inserted herself between us and grabbed the pencil case away from me. She held the pencil case up as she shook her hand and said in a loud tone, "This is Ingrid's pencil case." She went back and took her seat at the table while holding the pencil case tightly. Patrice's mom said quietly, "Ok, don't worry about it." Meanwhile, my mother kept repeating over and over that I should return the pencil case to Patrice at school the following day. Mama looked at her as usual, rolled her eyes and said, "This is not that lil gal's pencil case. I was right there when Ingrid buy this," as she lifted and squeezed the pencil case above her head. My mother said, "You spoiling Ingrid." She lunged and grabbed hold of the pencil case. There was a tug-of-war for my pencil case. Mama won the war. She got up and placed the pencil case on my bookshelf, and yelled at my mother and said, "Leave it right here." By this time, they squished the pencil case into a pulp.

Isn't that something? My mother believed in her friend's child and not her daughter. She was willing to give away something that belonged to me to satisfy her friend but didn't care about my feelings or that I would be without my pencil case and writing tools. I cannot find the words to explain this. All I know was it presented another moral dilemma. Patrice and I never spoke again. Another friend lost! Adults send mixed messages which may be conflicting to a child. I became confused as I tried to figure out what was going on and if there were any guidelines or rules for friendships. I was awakened to the fact that adults create their world of biases and gray areas that affect friendships both young and old.

Childhood Struggles for Education

Education is important and plays a vital role in our success. The process of its attainment can be very difficult and daunting for the less fortunate, who must work arduously through the maze of information and adaptations to satisfy our insatiable appetites for learning?

Mine was filled with childhood struggles, fantasies and hope for a bright future somewhere over the rainbow.

This is the story of my childhood struggles to get an education while growing up in Guyana on the South American Continent. However, these struggles are not typical of every Guyanese since we were all raised under different circumstances and socio-economic factors. The education system in Guyana differed from that in the United States. After my grandmother took me from my mother (when I was about eight years old), we went to live in New Amsterdam where she enrolled me in Mission Chapel Congregational School, named after the church that was next door. This primary (elementary) school was superb. I met the most amazing educators there. They were all interested in their students' wellbeing and success. I spent a few weeks in Standard Two; then I was transferred to Standard Three where I remained for the rest of the school year.

Academics were no problem for me. I received many awards for academics and good conduct. Standards Four to Five was when most students wrote the national exam called Common Entrance Exam to enter secondary school, also called high school. A good grade here would ensure a scholarship and acceptance into one of the country's top high schools. There were other high schools that accepted lower grades. However, only a chosen, special few students were given the opportunity to write this exam and be awarded scholarships to go to top-ranked high schools free. However, only the tuition was free. Parents purchased school uniforms and textbooks. I was not so fortunate to be selected to write this exam, even with my excellent grades and awards. I did not know or understand what the criteria for this selection process were. I know that many of the students who went to the top high schools came from the higher echelon in the community and some parents who could afford to pay the high tuition for their children. Everyone accepted it as the norm. I had to pursue a more difficult path.

After Standard Six, one would think according to the natural progression of classes, the next stage would be Standard Seven. However, there was no Standard Seven. The next class was Form One. This continued up to Form Six. Most students left school between Forms Four and Five. Form One marked the beginning of high school, while the end was between Forms Five and Six. A student could have spent between seven and eight years in primary school and four to six years in high school. Nursery school was not a requirement. A student could have left high school as early as age sixteen when he/she had completed the required courses and have written the General Certificate Exam (ordinary level).

I continued until I got to Standard Six where I could write other national exams that were less recognized. These exams were Preliminary Certificate Exam (P.C.). A passing grade in this exam allowed you to get into a lesser known or recognized high school. Then the College of Preceptors Exam (C.P.) which allowed students to write individual subjects such as Arithmetic, Geometry, English, Religious Knowledge and so on. This was also another path to high school and gave students between the ages of sixteen and eighteen the option to further their education by applying for training as an assistant teacher or nurse or find other employment. A passing grade would also allow a student to attend the Technical Institute. This marked the end of a student's life at the elementary level. The students also had another choice, which was to go to secondary school. There was no minimum or maximum age requirement to attend or leave elementary or high school, nor was there an age requirement to write the (P.C. nor C.P.) exams.

Attendance at high school was not a requirement. Many students did not attend high school because of the high cost of tuition. Also, students had other choices after leaving elementary school. These included trade school, technical institute, work, apprenticeship, or commercial school. This system may seem very confusing or archaic, but it worked.

They have changed this education system to one that is more inclusive. Every child now has an equal opportunity to write the Common Entrance Exam to enter high school, regardless of their socio-economic background. Even though the high schools are still ranked, each child has the same privilege to attend high school, according to a point value system coupled with the average points received at the exam. All government-controlled institutions from elementary school to University were tuition-free by the time I exited high school.

I passed both exams in primary school by the time I was fourteen. However, regardless of my situation, I wanted to go to high school to write the GCE-General Certificate Examination–Ordinary Level. They sent these exams from England. None of these exams were free. I paid for them using my savings in a tin can. The GCE – Ordinary Level was equivalent to a high school diploma in the US. Students were required to pass with good grades - A or B (along with five subjects at one sitting, including English and Math or six or more subjects at two sittings). After high school, students also had the opportunity to either go to Teachers' College, the Technical Institute or the University of Guyana or land a decent job in the public or private sectors. Alphabetical grades were not given in the regular school exams. Instead, students were given a numerical grade and ranked according to the grades received.

At the elementary school level, the older girls went to the home economics center once a week to learn various housekeeping skills while the boys went to the woodworking school to learn carpentry. Some teachers prepared students to write national exams by offering free lessons, called tutoring, in the afternoons after school and sometimes on the weekends. Some teachers even opened their homes to some of us for extra classes on the weekends, including Sundays without charging a fee. If many students would be present, then classes were held in school instead on the weekends. I was always present whenever and wherever classes were offered. All of my teachers did an excellent job of teaching and preparing us to write these exams.

This brings me to an ingenious way in which I got my education as a child. Since I had no mother and father to support my efforts—I only had an old and hardworking grandmother—it was imperative for me to make my mark in this world. One day, as I was playing under the stoop (also called a landing or porch), I saw my friend Jacqueline looking down at me from her window. She lived in the neighboring yard. I invited her to play. She said she could not come downstairs to play with me. Almost immediately, something happened. I cannot explain to this day what it was, but I picked up my bag of toys, went upstairs, threw them in the corner and sat down all alone.

I felt rage, disappointment, anger, confusion, and rejection once again. Maybe it was how Jacqueline spoke. I cannot explain my emotional state at this time. I did not think anyone could experience these emotions at the same time. I'm sure I did. As I sat there in my bewilderment, I thought to myself, "Why doesn't anybody like me?" By this time, I had experienced so much rejection I did not know what to do with myself— from my mother, who treated me differently from the rest of "her children"; my father, who preferred to go out of his way to visit my godmother and passed by my home and never came to see me but once; my dark skin, which seemed to be a repellant (whenever my sister and I were out in public, many adults would gravitate towards her because of her fair complexion and they left me standing there as though I were a leper); my god sisters who often said, "Ingrid is going to punish." but never gave me an explanation. Anyway, I knew it meant that I was doomed for a life of punishment or hardship. Even my Sunday school teacher, who did not want her granddaughter to speak to me when I did nothing wrong. I was only a child growing up in the ghetto. The one thing I knew for sure was that I had to do well. I had to carve out a better life for myself; one in which I would be respected and not feel rejected, dejected, ashamed, and alone. I would not live in the ghetto, nigger yard or tenement yard or whatever derogatory terminology was used to describe my living conditions when I grew up.

This tenement yard has several little houses, each comprising of three rooms–a kitchen, living room, and bedroom. A family of two or more people lived in each house. There were also outhouses and one community bathroom, along with one standpipe in the yard for everyone to use. There was no running water in the houses, except one. All the houses and amenities were in one small area in the yard. This style of living was also referred to as "The nigger yard" regularly. I did not know the history behind this offensive terminology. It embarrassed me to live here especially when I visited my friends who lived in better neighborhoods and I was too ashamed to invite them to my home. I had to correct this situation when I grew up.

I remembered what Mama kept saying, "Get an education, then you would not have to depend on no man for nothing." She said this repeatedly. I wondered why she was saying this to me when I was only a child. At this point, my mind wandered to my surroundings. The women in this yard might not have completed an elementary level of education. The men, whether working or not, took full advantage of the women. The men physically abused the women daily to the point of hospitalization and deformity. I did not know if any laws protected women from abuse. All I knew was that the men beat the women to a pulp. Some women would be absent for a few days, then when they reappeared, they were in bandages and walked crooked. There were endless fights coupled with the colorful language in cursing, sometimes all day long. The police came often. I guess they were accustomed to it. They knew my neighbors by name and could predict who started the fight. After a while, they made no arrests; they talked to them and left. Then, there would be peace for a little while, perhaps four or five hours, then the saga continued again, like a sequel in a soap opera. The young women left elementary school and worked the streets. Some of them got pregnant and bore children out of wedlock, while some got abortions. Whatever the situation was, they continued in the tradition of ghetto living. There were no betrothals or weddings here. Men and women just "shacked up."

I was exposed to another way of life. I visited rich people's homes, either when my grandmother worked there or with my god sisters on Sunday afternoons after Sunday school. I also went camping with other children from a higher socio-economic background. My grandmother taught me how to eat with knives and forks and set the table and sit and eat the correct way. She taught me good etiquette, table manners, and how to conduct myself in public or, as she would say, "among people." I impressed people everywhere I went. This was the life I wanted for myself. This was my destiny, and I would pursue it. I abhorred ghetto living.

What was I going to do about it? How am I going to get out of here? Where could I go? Who could I turn to for help? Could I get out of here? My ten-year-old brain became a minefield, about to explode with a multitude of questions that had no conceivable answers. Then, I remembered seeing young ladies attending commercial school during the day and in the afternoons. This was an 'aha' moment for me. 'The light bulbs came on and I was at home paying attention.' I thought commercial school would help me.

When my grandmother came home that evening, I told her I wanted to go to Commercial School in the afternoons after school. I thought this would be my passport out of the ghetto. This school taught Pitman's English, Typewriting and Shorthand. It prepared young men and young women to work in a business setting, doing secretarial work. Mama said, "all right," without giving it a second thought, and she said she would talk to Aunt Maggie, who was the school owner the following day. Aunt Maggie, as they fondly called her, had prepared many young women and a few men to be successful secretaries and clerks in offices. She was the best in her training and profession.

I had already figured out how I would pay for this school. My uncle Andy (Mama's son) sent money for her every week. I would save my allowance (called a pocket piece) every week in a clean, dry, empty tin-can, which was available. (Mama always saved cans.) Then, when we sold eggs and chickens (Mama reared chickens under the house, while my younger sister, Carol played with them) I would save some of that money too and leave the rest to buy food for the chickens and groceries for us. Also, if any money was left over from the market on Saturdays, I would put that in the tin-can. This was my great financial plan.

I had to wait a few months for the start of the new semester. I was about eleven years old when I started Pitman's Commercial School in the afternoons, while I attended elementary school during the day. Sometimes, I had to stay after school with the other students for tutoring before going to the commercial school. My plan worked. There was always money for my tuition and some leftover.

Meanwhile, as I was growing, I needed nice clothes like the other girls. One day I loosened one of my old dresses to see how it was sewn together. Then, I went to the fabric store and asked the saleslady how much cloth I needed to make a dress. She told me, and I bought the cheapest cotton (3 yards for $1.00), went home and cut my dress out (a little bigger), using the old dress as a pattern. I sewed it on my grandmother's old sewing machine, and it worked. This was the beginning of my dressmaking career. My grandmother no longer had to pay a dressmaker to get my clothes sewn. I used that money to make my own dresses. I could even buy shoes and socks. I saved the money that was leftover. Mama could not afford to buy "ready-made" clothes for us.

My neighbor (who lived in the front house), Mr. James, remarried after his wife's death. His new wife, Ms. Irene, was a dressmaker. I forged a relationship with her. I went over to help her on Friday afternoons and some Saturdays, to hem and baste clothes for her customers. She showed me how to measure and cut dresses the correct way, without using patterns. I loved to sew and dress up, but I did not want to make this my career. I sewed all of my clothes, even my grandmother's. When I learned to do smocking (special embroidery stitches) in school, I smocked some of my dresses and blouses. Everyone loved my smocked clothes. One day my aunt's friend brought some white satin material and thread and asked me to smock a dress for her baby's christening. I not only smocked the dress, but I also sewed the baby's dress with beautiful puffed sleeves. I also made the bonnet (hat). When Ms. Jem came to pick up the dress, it surprised her. She almost went into instant shock to see her baby's dress. I can still remember seeing her lifting the dress and turning it around as she touched the smocked areas. She kept asking, "Did you do this by yourself, Buggie? It's so clean and beautiful." It was a picturesque, long flowing white satin dress with white smocking around the neck and shoulders and at the end of the short-puffed sleeves. I did the scalloped lace trim around the top of the neck and at the end of the sleeves and dress hem. I made the bonnet with the leftover white satin material and some leftover white lace I had on hand. I trimmed the lace around the brim of the bonnet, and I made a beautiful bow to tie under the baby's chin. She gave me $20.00. This was my biggest payday so far. I went straight to my tin-can and deposited the money. I hid the tin-can behind my bookshelf.

Later, as my skills improved, I made dresses for brides and bridesmaids. I also made curtains, chair covers, finger and dish towels, cushions, sheets, and pillowcases, and costumes. I even tried making a bathing suit for myself. Later, when I left Guyana, I learned to use patterns to make my dresses. Somehow, I stopped sewing because of several reasons. Some of my clients did not want to pay, some underpaid me, and the most important part was my education. I went back to school to work on my BS degree and more. Also, I was active in church work. To this day, whenever I see a beautiful dress, I not only admire it, I think about the type of "cut," the material, the seams, the waistline, the hemline, how the pieces were put together and so on. I look at beautiful dresses in nostalgia and sometimes wished I had continued sewing.

One day my mother showed up with her sewing machine to exchange it for my grandmother's machine. She said her machine was heavy, and it hurt her chest whenever she used it. This was an almost new machine, so we made an exchange. Several months later, she returned to get her machine without Mama's machine. I told her she needed to return Mama's machine because she could not leave our house without a sewing machine and that I needed to use it. She said nothing and left. A few hours later, I heard a knock on the door. When I opened the door, she was standing there with a policeman. She told him I had her sewing machine. Mama said nothing; she sat there and rolled her eyes as she often did whenever something was out of order. Mama and the policeman told me to give it to her. I did so. When they left, I cried and cried because I loved to sew and now, I had no sewing machine.

To this day, I cannot believe a mother would do that to her child; moreover, to bring a police officer on her twelve-year-old child who had done nothing wrong. I continued to sew, but I had to do everything by hand. I learned to do different stitches in my sewing classes at school, so I now had to utilize this skill in my sewing. This was a slow and daunting process. We could not afford to buy another sewing machine at this time. However, a few months later, Uncle Andy bought me a new sewing machine. It was difficult for me to sew his pillow cases and bed sheets as well as patch his working pants without a sewing machine.

My mother repeated this action several years later. I was away in college when my mother returned to exchange sewing machines again. My grandmother allowed her to take my sewing machine while she left hers. It was old by this time. When I came home from college, my sewing machine was gone. My mother came again for the third time, asking for her sewing machine. I promptly asked her to return mine first. She once again left and showed up a few hours later with a policeman. Guess what? History just repeated itself all over again. I gave it to her in the name of peace. A few months later, I bought another sewing machine. This time it was not portable. I also let my mother know if she removed it from Mama's house for any reason, the tables will be turned and I did not care what the outcome would be. I was furious. I do not know how a parent could be so unfair and selfish. God knows I cannot write what I was thinking, so I will leave it alone.

Back to my money-making efforts: I joined the School Thrift Society at school. This allowed students to save money weekly. Each student had a savings book where we recorded our savings. The teacher in charge of the School Thrift Society also kept his/her records of our savings. Some of us (students) even raised funds on Fridays by making homemade ice cream and cakes. The students had 1½ hours for lunch, so we had adequate time to prepare our snacks. We shared the money equally and saved it in the School Thrift Society. We could not access this money until we left school. Some students left with hundreds of dollars. I only had about $100.00 because I had other things to do with my money.

My "hard, nappy hair" was a problem. Whenever my aunt washed my hair, she yanked it so hard that I screamed so loudly, you could hear me from a mile away. She did not stop or even paused until she was finished washing, drying, and combing my hair. We did not have a hairdryer, so even drying it with a towel made my head hurt. To this day, I still have pains in the middle of my head from all the yanking. Mama eventually sent me to a hairdresser (Madam Thom) to get it washed and pressed.

I could only go on Saturdays to get my hair done after completing my chores, which included going to the market, washing clothes and hanging them on the line to dry, house-cleaning, scrubbing the stairs and sometimes cooking. Most of the women got their hair done on Saturdays. By the time I got to the hair salon, it was filled with patrons waiting to get their hair done. I had to wait a long time to get my hair done. Madam Thom also trained young women to become hairdressers. While I was waiting, I was also observing and taking in everything. After all, I had nothing else to do. During Christmas and other holidays, the salon was unusually filled with patrons. There weren't enough "hands" to go around. One day, I was feeling very bored. So, I asked Madam Thom if I could help her wash and dry some heads. She said, "You sure Buggie?" I said, "Yes ma'am." She observed as I washed and set my first head of hair. She said,

"Where did you learn to do this?" I said, "Right here ma'am." She had that puzzled look on her face as she said, "That's good." She allowed me to do a second and third head and so on. Then one day, a lady wanted her hair pressed in a hurry and no one was available. I said excitedly, "Can I do it Madam Thom?" She looked at me as though I were a crazy child about to get her in trouble. I said, "I'll show you." The lady sat quietly and entrusted her head in the hands of an amateur practitioner and a child "to add insult to injury." Not a smart move, but I was thankful. I started bravely, as I repeated every word, I heard Madam Thom say to her trainees. She stood there and looked dumbfounded as I demonstrated my skills. It was perfect and the beginning of another career—hairdresser. When I was not doing dressmaking with Ms. Irene, I went to Madam Thom to do hairdressing. My hairdressing skills also came in useful. Later, when I attended college, I made a good living doing hairdressing for some students and friends. I even washed, dyed, and pressed Mama's hair until she decided to surrender to nature's natural course—gray and natural hair. At that point, I did not want a career in hairdressing. I was just a very curious and enterprising child.

Back to Aunt Maggie's school: I went to classes from Monday to Thursday. I learned Pitman's Shorthand, Typing and English. I did this for one year. However, no one paid much attention to me in class. Maybe because I was the youngest student in the school and there were many students. Classes weren't taught in conventional groups. Each student was at a different point in the textbooks and therefore required individual attention. Much of what I learned was self-taught. My work was corrected by one teacher, who spent a few minutes teaching me individually as she did with other students. So, they couldn't spend much time helping each student. Then one afternoon my grandmother asked me if Aunt Maggie allowed me to write any exam. I said, "No." She told me I would not be going back to that school. Imagine my horror when I heard this. I thought I would take my last breath and die. I stood there, dumbfounded, and looked at her while I dare not say a word. She seemed furious. Then, after a lengthy pause, she said, "I will talk to Teacher Aileen tomorrow." My grandmother was not gifted with many words. She got straight to the point and then the end. I felt an immediate relief. Teacher Aileen had another commercial school, and Aunt Maggie also trained her.

When school reopened in the fall, September, I went to Victoria Commercial School. I was still the youngest in my classes again. The classes here were smaller, so I got more teacher-student attention. However, the structure was the same as Aunt Maggie's. By the end of the second semester in March, I was preparing to write exams in Elementary English and Typing and Theory Stage One Shorthand. The older girls who knew the system rented all the typewriters early. I told Mama what happened. She took me to Mr. Mendoza's shop. He repaired and sold typewriters. I examined most of the typewriters until I found the one I liked. I could see that Mr. Mendoza was getting impatient as he wondered what I was up to. He told my grandmother I was very inquisitive. This did not bother me. After all, my grandmother was paying for it, and it was my job to get her money's worth. I selected an Olympian typewriter, and it was 'fine.' The following day, I went to my tin-can and got enough money to pay for my exams.

Later, I learned that Mama had taken out almost all her money from the bank to purchase my first typewriter. This confirmed what I already knew—she loved and cared for me, even though she never told me. I knew it was my job to work hard to make her feel proud of me. I studied, wrote and passed all my exams. Mama said nothing, neither did she show any emotion. I knew she cared, anyway.

As a child, I never got hugs and kisses or any verbal encouragement, praises or affirmations. However, when I needed anything, I always got it. As a child, one could not tell that I was from the ghetto, if you did not know me. I presented myself differently by my speech, my deportment, mannerisms, and general appearance. My grandmother accepted nothing less from me. She always insisted that I do everything to the best of my ability. When the other children could run and play in the yard "bare feet," for example, I had to wear my "yard shoes," and I had to use my "house slippers" in the house. Even now, I think my feet are still softer than my hands.

I was very serious about my schoolwork and showed a lot of interest in my classes. Teacher Aileen always used me as an example when she wanted to showcase a conscientious student to the older girls. She referred to me as "this little girl." Then, one day when she made her usual remarks, she "was getting on my last nerves." I said under my breath, "I am not a little girl." She heard me. She then changed it to "this big girl." I knew I couldn't win, so I left it alone.

There were three semesters in one school year. I wrote and passed all of my exams. By the end of this school year, I achieved many academic awards including Proficiency in Typewriting. I attended this school the following year with continued success. By the time I was fourteen, I had Pitman's Elementary, Intermediate and Advanced Typing and English. My typing speed was ninety-two words per minute. My shorthand speed was one hundred twenty words per minute. This was quite an accomplishment for a fourteen-year-old.

Even though I was a smart and enterprising child, one would think my family would be proud of me. This was not the case. When my aunt learned that I was going to a commercial school, she became adamant and very vindictive. She told my grandmother that "you do not waste money on other people's children." She told my mother Mama she was wasting her money on me and she did not send them to learn anything, and that I would be ungrateful. My mother agreed with her and was furious. She even stopped sending me her occasional packages of clothing. I did not care because they did not fit well, anyway. I had to alter them to suit my taste. Mama told me to just ignore them; they never wanted to learn anything when they were children. She told me stories about my mother and her siblings. My mother started piano lessons when she was a child and quit soon after. According to my mother, the piano teacher wiped the keys after she was finished playing but did not do the same with the other children. She felt badly and quit. My aunt and one uncle did nothing but fight with other students almost daily. The only one who did something with his life was my youngest uncle who went to commercial school and later opened his commercial school when he got married and moved to the Essequibo Coast. My other uncle attended a trade school after he left school.

My aunt gave me more chores to do every day. When I did not do them to her specifications, she would hit me with sticks, pot spoons, and rolling pins—anything she got her hands on—and pulled my hair. To this day, I have marks on my skin and pain in the center of my head because of her abuse. Many times, when she got enraged, I would run to the backyard, jump over the trench (also called a ditch) and hide in the cemetery until she left or Mama came home. Sometimes I would be there for several hours. Don't worry, there were many fruit trees such as coconuts, tamarind, mangoes and jamun and lots of shade in the cemetery. I climbed the trees and got my full supply of fruits there. I even had my special tomb that I sat on. I was not afraid of anything. There was only one tomb close to our yard. The other tombs were far away.

I used to play in the cemetery with some children in the neighborhood when I was much younger. We used to climb the trees and pick the fruits. We left a cutlass there so it would be convenient for us to cut coconuts and wood to make a fire for our "bush cook" or cookout. We took ingredients from our parents/guardian's home along with old pots, pans, plates, and spoons to make up our desired cuisine for the day. These dishes were delicious, of course; we cooked them nice and smoky flavored.

Whenever I ran out of the house, my aunt thought I was going to the duplex at the backyard and that I would become a whore. She told my uncle who left his home in Mackenzie and had to travel for several hours to come to Mama's house and beat me. She never came to look for me. If she did, she would have known I was not there but hiding in the cemetery instead. Mama told me not to go to the house in the backyard, so I never went there. I had a special tomb I sat on and read whenever I could grab a book on my way out. This happened at least once every two weeks.

My aunt made life very difficult for me. She knew school started at 8.30 in the morning. Just when I was getting dressed to go to school, she made me scrub the front and back stairs in an effort to make me tardy.

Somehow, I knew she would demand clean stairs so I got ahead of her and did it in the evening. The next morning before she made her demands, I told her the steps were already scrubbed. She yelled and said, "scrub de kitchen." I stopped dressing, got my bucket, filled it with water, got the scraper and floor cloth, and went to work. Needless to say, I was late for school that morning. I felt like Cinderella, but without the fairy godmother. She knew now that I did my daily chores in the evenings. Whenever she came home at nights, instead of wiping her feet on the mat or folded bag that was placed at the bottom of the steps, she just walked past it and went straight upstairs carrying the mud with her, thereby making it necessary for me to scrub the stairs in the mornings. May God help me if it rained. I just could not win so I got up earlier in the mornings to do my chores. We had the cleanest steps in the yard. One morning Mama did not go to work because she was not feeling well. When she saw me cleaning, she asked what I was doing; I told her Tita told me to clean before I went to school. She said, "Stop this damn stupidness. Go and put on your clothes for school." I immediately pushed the bucket with water and floor cloth to the edge of the steps, ran to the pipe and washed my hands. I felt such a relief. My morning chores were now over.

As I was getting dressed for school, I heard Mama and Tita arguing loudly. I did not pay any attention to them; I knew they were fussing over me. I got dressed quickly, picked up my bag, and ran out the door. This time I was early for school. I was never accosted to do morning cleanings again.

Meanwhile, I could not do my homework or study early in the evening, so I went to bed early. There was too much noise and ruckus in the house, made by my aunt when she was at home, but somehow, I managed to get some sleep. She turned up the volume of the radio. Every movement she made was loud. She called me frequently to do something that was unnecessary. As a result, I woke up in the wee hours of the mornings, about one to two o'clock when it was nice and quiet to study and do my homework. I was determined that nothing or no one would impede my success. I would allow no one to put out the little flicker of my candlelight. I was determined to push through until I achieved my goals. I refused to allow anyone to bulldoze my plans or use a wrecking ball to destroy my future because of their ignorance or jealousy.

Even though an educational achievement should be celebrated, rewarded and most of all announced, I could not let my aunt or mother know of my own achievements for fear of their harsh reprisal. I kept it to myself. Only my grandmother knew of my success.

I must note at this point that my aunt was not always indifferent towards me. I remembered being with her at age five or six. She took good care of me. Mama gave me a bicycle which she got from her employer when she worked in Watooka. Tita taught me to ride my bicycle. When I fell, she picked me up and told me to try again. She took care of my bruises and cuts. She did my laundry, cooked, and baked. She even represented me when adults and children tried to take advantage of me. The only problem I had with her was when she washed my hair. She only became very abusive when she learned that I would attend commercial school and then high school. I believe she wanted me to continue in the family tradition of being domestic servants or maids while living and struggling in the ghetto. She believed I was not suitable for commercial school and that this school was only for rich students.

Meanwhile, I had no peace with the neighbors in the yard. They cursed and called me names daily, including queen, bitch, and whore. Even the adults joined in. What made matters worse was that I was allergic to mosquito bites. Whenever I scratched, the bumps turned into sores. Mama used to rub my skin with many funny-smelling mixtures at nights, but nothing worked. She burned mosquito coils at night to keep away the mosquitoes. She even bought me a mosquito net to protect me while I slept. We had to close our windows early before 7 p.m. so that the mosquitoes could not come into the house. Nothing worked. So, my other nickname became "mangy." No one would believe I once played with these children with no problems. I stopped playing because I had to go to commercial school in the afternoons and on the weekends, I was engaged in other activities such as hairdressing or sewing. Apart from this, I was also getting ahead of myself—too grown and too sophisticated to get involved in childish activities. I had better things to do with my time.

On one occasion, while I was bathing in the community bathroom, one of the young men came into the bathroom to rape me. I had to fight for my life and I clamped down on his arm and bit him really hard. He ran out of the bathroom screaming. Even though he could not rape me, he taunted me every day. One of the young women, Charlotte, said she would beat me up. I do not know what her motivation was; I did not do anything to her. My grandmother went to an attorney, Marcelle (who was also her nephew). He sent her a letter to cease and desist. She stopped her threats while the others laughed whenever I passed by. This went on for several years.

This was a troublesome time for me during the beginning stages of my adolescent journey. I was questioning my identity and the purpose of my existence. For example, my nickname was "Buggie." I wanted nothing to do with this name. I saw my birth certificate, and this name was not there. I did not want to be called out of my name. I was already carrying the last name of a man I did not know and whom I believed did not want me to be a part of his life. I also thought he had disowned me while his name was still on my birth certificate.

Imagine my frustration when I asked my grandmother why I had to use his name and she said she wanted me to know who my father was! This explanation was mindboggling till today because I still do not know who my father was. They told me I "resembled" him, with his wide gap between his front teeth and other spaced teeth, and dark complexion. This was no comfort to me. So, what…if I wanted to know who my father was, should I go look in a mirror? Or, since I looked like him, maybe I could pick him out in a crowd! What a consolation!

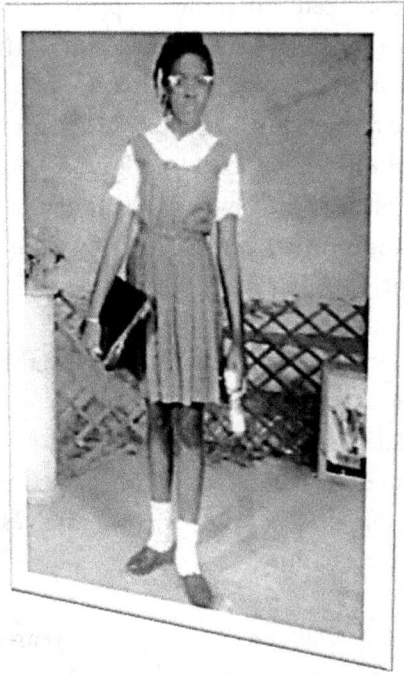

My 14th Birthday

I am wearing my school uniform I made.
I purchased my books, briefcase, pencil case, socks
& shoes with the money I earned.

Anyway, let's continue with my identity formation. When anyone in the yard called me "Buggie," I promptly reminded them that my name was Ingrid. I had to assert my identity in the metamorphosis of my life. As a matter of fact, I did not know the origin or significance of this name. Some adults thought it was cute to shorten my nickname to "Buggs." This irritated me even more. Eventually, I stopped answering to this name. This infuriated them because they thought I was rude and disrespectful to them. They complained to my grandmother. Mama said to them, "Her name is Ingrid." This brought the name calling to an end. "Oh, what a relief!"

When I turned fourteen, my father stopped paying for child support through the courts because I was a bastard child. That was the law and, therefore, legal at that time. My mother came home and brought me a wristwatch and some money. She had allowed the money to accumulate in the courts for several months. She did not give Mama any of this money for me. As a matter of fact, she never gave Mama any money for me. Up to this point, my grandmother was struggling with me all by herself, with a little help from Uncle Andy.

I wonder just what the British lawmakers were thinking when this law was enacted. A fourteen-year-old child cannot find full-time employment to support him/her adequately, except for menial jobs with low wages. The legal age for employment was eighteen. At this age (fourteen) a child could not gain any employable skills, nor support themselves independently. This seemed to be a set up for failure.

The questions are, what makes a fourteen-year-old bastard child so different from a fourteen-year-old child born in wedlock? We were all God's children. We did not ask to be born. We were the product of irresponsible people. Maybe if adults would be more mindful of their social and sexual activities, then bastardization would not be a source of inconvenience and embarrassment for them. Further, there would not be any unplanned pregnancies and fatherless children. Also, since my father still had his legitimate fourteen-year-old child and older children living in his precious household, was I not worthy of the same support? What was I supposed to do without his support? This was mindboggling! It defies human logic that an illegitimate child could be treated differently because of the nature of his/her conception, while they treated a child born in wedlock with the utmost care, love and respect until the age of maturity (eighteen years) and even longer if the child is in school. That was indeed an unjust system.

I was ready to leave primary school by age fourteen anyway. I finished early because I skipped two classes and passed all of my exams. There was nowhere else for me to go, or nothing else for me to do here. I did not want to wait until I was older to become an assistant teacher at this time. I wanted to go to secondary school. This would be a challenge for me. There were no public high schools, and private high school was more expensive than a commercial school.

Once again, I had a plan. Since I already had advanced certificates, I could stop commercial school and save for high school instead. Also, I typed for my grandmother's friends and others who passed by and heard my loud typewriter in action. They recommended me to their friends because I did an excellent job for them. I used to read and correct their letters before I typed them. More money was coming in this way. Madam Thom also gave me some money for helping out in her salon. I also had savings in the School Thrift Society and in my tin-cans. Uncle Andy was still making weekly contributions to Mama.

Early one morning before school started, I walked up to the high school (Berbice Educational Institute) and asked for the principal. I expressed my desire to attend this school. He told me to bring my certificates for him to see. I said "alright" and I left. He never asked for my parents or how was I going to pay the tuition. That evening when Mama came home, I told her what I did. In my enthusiasm, I seemed to put the cart before the horse. This was a very bold move. Mama paused and said, "I don't know what I'm gonna do with you." Another long pause, then she said, "We will go to BEI next week." Thinking that she was trying to dismiss me I asked, "Which day?" By this time, she was heading for the kitchen. She turned around and rolled her eyes and said, "I gon tell yo." Pressing the issue further and looking for a positive outcome, I said, "I have the money to pay." She continued towards the kitchen and said, "Next week." Mama could be a hard woman to convince sometimes, but I was persistent. That evening, during dinner, I outlined my plans to her. Since I already had advanced certificates in typing and English, I could leave commercial school. The only thing I could do here was shorthand speed. I convinced her that I really wanted to go to high school. This would help me to get a better position when I searched for a job. She agreed, and I was relieved. The following week we went to BEI, and I was enrolled. Instead of starting at Form One, I would start in Form Four. I felt as though I was walking on clouds.

Dr. Ingrid J. Benjamin Ph.D.

Off to High School

*I paid the first term (semester) – three months tuition from
my savings. I also bought my tie and accessories, books
and uniform material with the money I saved.
I made my own uniform, including the shirts.*

When I started high school, I had enough money in my savings to purchase my books, pay my tuition for the first semester, purchase material for my school uniform and other supplies for school. By this time, we had gotten another sewing machine, so I sewed my school uniform. I made puffed sleeve shirts instead of the regular sleeves. When my mother saw my shirts, she said that they would put me out of the school because that was not the uniform. This did not happen, however. Everyone loved my modestly puffed sleeves. When Uncle Andy came to visit Mama, he showed me how to fix my tie.

When my aunt heard that I was heading for high school, she became even more enraged again. She told all of her friends that Mama was spoiling me and wasting her money and that I would be ungrateful. She kept repeating this over and over to Mama, like a broken record. My grandmother did what she always did—rolled her eyes, hissed her teeth and ignored her.

The transition to high school was a challenge for me. It differed greatly from elementary school. I was shocked to find out that there was a teacher for each subject. The workload was heavy because each teacher gave his/her homework, and classes stuck to a regular schedule. They gave each student individual schedules of his/her classes. Students were addressed differently. The boys were called by their last names while the girls were called Miss and their last names. (Example Miss Benjamin.) This school was ranked the second best in our Region. I was placed in Form Four. This was equivalent to a junior (grade eleven here in the USA). There were six Forms in some of our top high schools. Form Five would be equivalent to the Senior Year or Grade Twelve. The Sixth Form would be equivalent to the first year of college here in the USA. Very few students stayed long enough to enter the Sixth Form. Not all high schools had the Sixth Form though. Most high schools stopped at Form Five. Students who entered the Sixth Form wrote the GCE advanced level, another exam that came from England.

Most students left high school between the Fourth and Fifth Forms. This meant that they were between the ages of sixteen and eighteen. Some students pursued higher education in Teachers' College, University of Guyana, the Technical Institute, Nursing School or did apprenticeship training at a job site, while others just hung around until they were ready to make that crucial decision about their lives.

There were no high school graduations as those held in the USA. Graduations were only held at the university level. There was only an award ceremony at the end of the school year in college. The elementary and high schools had an awards ceremony at the end of each term (semester). There were no proms or organized sports teams. Even Physical Education was optional, and that was held in the afternoons after school or early in the mornings before school. I did not play an active role in sporting events. However, I supported my athletic friends in their endeavors which was held only one day during the school year, when there were track and field competitions with other schools. I was too cute to sweat. This activity was not for me. I had no intention to run anywhere or jump anything.

I attended Berbice Educational Institute, a predominately East Indian high school. Other races were in the minority. The students and teachers were outstanding. I made friends with four incredible young ladies. They were Phyllis and Donna who lived on the Corentyne and commuted daily. This made it difficult for us to associate after school. We talked after classes and when I got back to school after the lunch break. My other friends were Maureen and Ingrid. They lived in my hometown. We walked home every day after school. My grandmother gave them her seal of approval. According to her, they came from "good stock." This meant that their parents were outstanding citizens in the community. In case you were wondering, my grandmother chose my friends for me. She always said, "Show me your company and I'll tell you who you are." Ingrid's father was in the military. He had a band for young people. She encouraged me to join the band. After careful consideration, I decided not to join. It was not cost effective for me since I already had other monetary commitments. I had to purchase my musical instrument and uniforms for the band. I also had to invest a lot of time in the afternoons to attend practice sessions. This would have been in direct conflict with my commercial school, and I was trying to complete my program at the end of that semester. With my limited exposure, I didn't think that being in a band and music would benefit me in the future. I had to remain focused on my goal.

My friends and I could not spend much time together outside of school. My grandmother had a tight leash on me. I could not go to the cinema or parties because of church rules. I could only go camping with adult supervision. I enjoyed my high school days since they gave me something to look forward to. It gave me hope. All my friends had dreams, or as my grandmother would have said, "Ambition." Donna and Phyllis wanted to be teachers. Maureen wanted to be a nurse like her mother. Ingrid wanted to be in banking with her older sister. I wanted to be a secretary or teacher; whichever one would take me out of the ghetto faster! As a teenager, I just couldn't identify with my living situation. It was embarrassing and very demeaning. I had to find a way out.

Meanwhile, I still had to study and do my homework in the wee hours of the mornings. My aunt was relentless and determined not to leave me alone because she did not want me to succeed. The courses in high school were relatively easy except for chemistry and physics; There were just too many courses. If I were to become a success, I had to work harder and try to keep up. Since physics and chemistry were challenging to me, I put more effort into them and studied harder, because I had not done them before.

The most amazing and incredible phenomenon happened to me in high school. This was a supernatural experience. One night, I went to bed very perplexed and worried that I was having a hard time with physics. In my dreams, I saw a "white" handwriting on a blackboard. When I looked carefully, it was the steps to solve my physics problems. I heard no voice and saw no physical form of a body; I did not even see a face. I only saw the handwriting, the step-by-step illustrations and instructions on the blackboard. This continued throughout my high school years, not every night though. Whenever I was having a problem in math, physics or chemistry, I went to bed and my tutoring session began. I was not afraid, and I told no one until now. Coupled with this experience, sometimes when I slept, I would see a movie of my activities the following day. The activities of the entire day would be revealed to me. For example, whenever there was a surprise test (also called a pop quiz), I would see the subject and the questions, but no answers, so I knew what to study when I awoke early in the morning. However, I never saw a planned test. Once again, I never told a single soul because I did not want anyone to think I was crazy or describe me negatively. My mother already said that I would "run off" or go crazy if I did not stop studying.

During my tenure in high school, there were many challenges. Sometimes when a teacher was absent, there were no substitutes. They left the students to fend for themselves. When this occurred, all of us got into groups and reviewed our work. In most cases, the answers were at the back of the textbook and this was helpful. I remember when our Economics teacher quit, and there was no replacement. We got together, and each student studied parts of the text and taught the class during that period. We were not fortunate to have substitute teachers or anyone to supervise us whenever a teacher was absent. If we would be successful, then we had to make it happen for ourselves. We studied and worked hard together whenever a teacher was absent. There was no fooling around or horseplay during our classes. We took the quizzes and tests from the back of the textbooks. We exchanged test papers and graded them. Talk about honesty. It appears the students in my classes were all kindred souls, with an insatiable appetite for learning and with well-defined goals for success.

It appears most of the students in my high school were on a mission. They came from very far away to attend school. Some students were up as early as four o'clock in the mornings to catch a bus. The bus could only take them so far, and then they had to take a taxi or walk the rest of the way to school. Some students came from across the Berbice River–from Rosignol or Blairmont, which meant that they had to wait for the Torani, an ancient and slow steamer (boat). It was often off schedule and late. Some students took launches (small boats) to cross the Berbice River from Blairmont. Either way, students made great sacrifices to attend school. Most students took between one and two hours to get to school and just about the same time to get back home. Some students came from the Corentyne coast and had to travel for at least one to two hours by bus each way, depending on how far they lived. As if this was not bad enough, all students, teachers and the residents in that area had to tread on a dirt road to get to their ultimate destination—school, work or home. In my case, I only had to walk to school, which was just up the road, less than a mile away. I even went home for lunch. May God help us when it rained! Wading and skipping and navigating through large puddles were an art form to be mastered if you wanted to keep your uniform and shoes clean. Many of us wore goulashes and long boots on rainy days. This was a great and daunting transportation challenge.

Some students took their lunches and snacks with them, while others went home for lunch, which was 1½ hours long. There were no cafeterias or lunchrooms in our school. Students took their lunches to school and ate in the classrooms. Imagine the odor in the classroom during lunchtime! Lunches were all homemade—cooked food from scratch, no sandwiches, no store-bought food and certainly, no fast foods. Fast foods were not available or even heard of at this time. A lot of families did not have gas or electric stoves. They cooked on kerosene oil stoves, coal pots or firesides—a very slow process. Imagine, students who lived far away had to get up early in the morning to cook food from scratch. Some parents got up early to cook. In most cases, we placed the food in thermal flasks to keep it hot (warm). My grandmother got up early in the morning to cook before she went to work. There were street vendors who sold snacks such as polouru, (pholourie) bara, channa, tamarind syrup (salt and sweet) and drinks such as mauby, swank (lemonade) and pine drink as well as fruits, at the side of the road. These snacks were in glass cases or displayed on a tray. It's unbelievable that some of us made it through high school with perfect attendance, on time, and with excellent grades.

Meanwhile, my aunt, still full of hatred and jealousy, brought a fat "dougla" man (half African and half East Indian descent) into the house. She told my grandmother that he would help me with my studies. She showed him to the bedroom and told me to follow him. I did as I was told. When I got into the bedroom, he told me to bend over, and I did. He immediately pulled my underwear to the side and tried to insert his penis into my vagina. When I felt the pain and pressure, I jumped and ran out of the room and told my grandmother. Mama immediately put him out.

When I went to the front door, my aunt was sitting on the steps peeping into the bedroom from a crease in the wall, to see what was happening. When she saw me, she became very adamant and said, "whaaw rang with yo?" As if I should have leaned over to let this grown man rape me. When she came inside, a heated argument ensued with my grandmother. This was the first time I saw my grandmother angry. She even told my aunt to get out of her house. I wished that my aunt would have left us alone and moved on with her life, but she stayed and continued with her evil ways.

When I thought about this incident, I often wondered about the condition of the human heart. What would warrant an adult to bring a grown man to rape or have sex with a fifteen-year-old child? Further, when that child was her niece—a close relative whom she held as a baby and cared for as a young child. One would think her primary responsibility was to protect that child from all harm and danger. Was it hate? Was it jealousy? Was it arrogance? Or just stupidity? Or did she want to destroy me so badly that she could not help herself? I know that she did it on purpose to hurt me. I also wondered why Mama allowed me to go into the bedroom with this man. Was she so over eager for me to succeed in school? I may never find the answers to these questions. Anyway, I have since forgiven them because this is the right thing to do since I am now a Christian.

After this incident, I became very resentful towards my aunt. The next time she tried to punish me without cause, I picked up a cutlass and told her if she hit me, I would chop her up. I meant every word. This came from many years of stored-up anger and rage that I just had to let go. I even stopped speaking to her. She left me alone and never threatened me again, nor imposed unnecessary chores and punishment on me.

However, she was never happy to see me at peace. Whenever she or any of her friends saw me talking to a boy, she would promptly inform Uncle Andy. He believed every word that she said and would come home and hit me without asking me about the problem. Somehow, I knew that he would hit me just before his departure to return to his home, so I ran to the cemetery and waited for him to leave. One day when he came to Mama's house, I asked him why he was always hitting me when I did nothing wrong. He told me he did not want me to end up like my mother, making children out of wedlock and being used by men. He wanted me to get an education and become a powerful woman. I said, "That's what I am doing. Please stop hitting me." I did not know he had such high hopes for me. This was the first time he expressed these positive sentiments to me. I showed him some of my awards and certificates. He was surprised. The hitting stopped. But he was always suspicious and protective of me. He even protected me through college by making surprise visits on the pretense of bringing me money and food. Later, when he learned more about my full achievements, he was very proud of me. He gave me everything I wanted and would never listen to my ignorant aunt again. He would often tell his friends very proudly, "That's my niece."

When my Mama got sick and could not go to work, Uncle Andy told her to stop working altogether. Without hesitation, she asked him, "What would happen to Ingrid?" He said that he would take care of me. "He put his money where his mouth was." Every week he sent a little more money for us. He paid for my trips, vacations, camps, and exams and just about everything I needed. I never had to struggle for anything after this point. However, I continued to save my money as usual. Mama always encouraged me to "save for a rainy day." She also kept saying to me, "Mother has, father has, blessed is the child who has his own." When I was much younger, I did not understand what these sayings meant, but as I grew older and faced my own issues, these words became more meaningful to me.

Meanwhile, Mama stayed at home and made more scrap-mats from my left-over sewing material called scraps. She also spent more time trying to get people to join her Self-Help Housing Scheme Project. She always said that when she left the ghetto (and sometimes she said, "Jill yard"-named after the landlord) she wanted to go into her own home. She thought this was the easiest and most affordable path towards home ownership.

I only spent two years in high school. I wrote the national exam which came from England. It was called The General Certificate of Examination, Ordinary Level (GCE O Level). I passed five subjects. This exam was equivalent to a high school diploma in the USA. I did not return to high school the following semester. Instead, I went to a tutor to get help to prepare to write a few more subjects at the GCE O Level. This was more economical than attending high school. I wrote the exam again, and I passed three more subjects. My high school days were over. I was now ready for the world, or so I thought!

MY SAVINGS PLAN

Every Week I saved some money in two tin-cans to pay for my tuition for commercial and high schools. I bought material to make my clothes, bought my schoolbooks and supplies, paid for my exams and anything else I needed. I hid my savings behind my books on the little two- shelf bookcase that was nailed to the wall.

I got money when we sold chickens and eggs, from my grandmother, from Aunty Carmen, from Uncle Andy, when I typed documents for my grandmother's friend, from Madam Thom and Ms. Irene. I also saved money in the School Thrift Society. I had many means of earning money.

Triumphs of a Little Girl

A handbag *A hand towel*

A Sample of crafts I have made as a child

A Scrap Mat

Mama made Scrap Mats from my left-over sewing materials called scraps. These mats could also be used on the floor, beds, chairs or displayed on walls. They were mainly used on the floor as a rug.

My Grandmother and Me

I am very blessed to be a part of my grandmother's militant but caring upbringing.

A disciplinarian to the core, yet one of the most forward-thinking individuals that have graced my life.

She was not just a beacon of light for me; she was the base on which my entire life revolved.

Mama took me in, stood like a strong tower and supported me against all odds.

She believed in me when no one else cared about me.

My social life at this point was fantastic. It was the flip side of my home life. My grandmother worked as a domestic servant and in stores and restaurants and in a hotel as a cook. She did whatever she had to do to support us. Even though we were poor, she sacrificed to give me everything I needed. She would rather let me have what I wanted while she went without.

Mama never kept me at home during the summer and Easter holidays. She often sent me away to the country to be with her niece, Aunt Dena, who was an unmarried teacher and was raising two of her own nieces. Here, I got to spend time with my older cousins who were beautiful young ladies. I loved country living. There were fruit trees in galore and most of all, I was unrestricted. I got to run free and spent most of the time outdoors, sometimes all day long. I got to be a "tomboy." I climbed the trees, picked the fruit, cut coconuts, and drank the water straight from the shell, then cut the nuts, made spoons from the shell and ate the jelly right out of the nut. I was totally free and uninhibited; what glorious times!

In the evenings, my cousins and I huddled together on the front steps and they talked about fashion, their boyfriends and other young men and women in the village, and sometimes ghost stories that scared me to death. Most afternoons they got "dolled" up and were forced to take me with them. They ambled along the village dam while their boyfriends waited on the side of the dam, close to the public road for them to arrive. They had to be far away from the house where Aunt Dena could not see them from her front porch (landing) where she spent most of her time. While they visited with their boyfriends, they gave me money to go to the corner shop to buy mauby (bitter/sweet drink) and cake. They instructed me to stay there until they were ready to get me. I did as they told me. However, I sat by the window where I got a perfect view of their activities. I saw all the kissing and playing behind the trees. Incidentally, this was my first lesson in being sneaky and making up stories, and I perfected this art form later—don't ask, it's coming!

We had to make it back home before it got dark—our curfew. The whole village got dark at night. There were no streetlights, except for the major road. The light of the stars and the full moon illuminated the sky and the entire village on a cloudless night.

The end of my vacation was like a slow funeral procession. I did not want to leave, and neither did Eve and Vesta. My leaving meant the end of their evening rendezvous with their boyfriends. They could only sneak to see them after school, on their way home. In other words, they used me as a pawn to see their boyfriends. I had to remember that I was going back home to Mama's house, where I had to speak softly and properly and wear a pair of house slippers inside the house and shoes when I was going outside to play or fetch water. My wildness was curtailed here. Otherwise, I would have to suffer the consequences. I remember the first time when I came back from the country. I was so eager to tell Mama how I spent my vacation. I began with a loud tone and "bad" speech. Mama stamped her feet on the ground and yelled at me. She startled me; she seemed furious. She said, "Stop right there, speak properly." I would not try that again. Now, Mama never spoke "the Queen's English" as she often said was good speech. Her English was not perfect either. However, I was required to speak perfectly. Mama knew whenever my speech was wrong, and she promptly corrected me. Sometimes, this was embarrassing because she did it in front of my friends.

Mama sometimes sent me to my uncle Urban, who lived on the Essequibo Coast. His wife, Aunty Carmen, introduced me to make-up and the world of cosmetics. She sold a popular line of cosmetic products. Whenever I was ready to return home, she gave me a bag of cosmetics, new clothes, a supply of sanitary pads, and money. Spending holidays with my aunt and uncle gave me a different experience. Aunty Carmen's younger sisters were closer to my age, so we played house and played other childhood games together. The Atlantic Ocean was not far away. We played at the edge of the Ocean and built mud houses. We were not allowed to climb trees. Uncle Urban and Aunty Carmen took me on many trips to the Mainstay lake and other parts of the Essequibo. We traveled throughout the Essequibo Coast. It was exquisite and breathtaking.

The only holiday I can remember spending at home with my grandmother was Christmas. When I was much older, fourteen to sixteen years old, she sent me to summer camps. Here I met other children from across the country. Some camps were academic, some were religious, and others were just fun. I also went to several school and church trips.

Spending holidays away from home was great fun. However, I had to get home at least one week before the holiday ended. Mama had a ritualistic process before school began for the next session. It's something she called, "purging." She gave me a dose of castor oil on the first day. If she thought I did not have enough "motions" or bathroom visits that day, I was given another dose the following day. Sometimes she mixed the castor oil with cassareep for maximum effect. Senna pods or senna leaves were soaked in hot water and strained. This was taken for the next three days. Then she said, "You had a good clean out." Meanwhile, I was in pain and agony for at least four days after the purging, not to mention the discomfort on my poor bottom. You see, most times we could not afford to use toilet paper. We used wet newspapers or wet brown paper. This "purging thing," may have worked. I never got sick as a child. When many of my classmates were home sick with the flu or other childhood diseases, I was strong and well. Yea Mama! I never kept up this ritual as an adult. I was done with that.

I must interject and mention a frightening experience I had while on a school trip to Georgetown, our capital when I was about eleven-years-old. While in primary school, they selected me to sing in our school choir. There was a competition among the elementary schools in the country. The choir was comprised of only girls. That night, we practiced, played games, fooled around and went to bed. The next morning when I awoke, it surprised me to find blood on my nightdress. I was terrified and did not know what to do. I heard the older girls saying something about a "young lady" but I did not understand what they were saying. I went to the bathroom to take a shower. To my surprise, as I disrobed, I saw blood on my underwear too. I was frightened and confused; I did not know what to do. I took a bath, folded my bloody clothing, and tucked them away in my bag. I said nothing to anyone. I got dressed for the competition and followed the direction of my teachers.

We went to the concert hall. The rest of the students sang their hearts out, except for me. I was too afraid to open my mouth. I forgot the words of the song. To this day, the only words of that song I can remember are something about Sir Walter Raleigh. Our choir was not selected to continue in the competition, so we left the city and returned home the same day. I ate nothing because I was afraid that I would get sicker.

As soon as I returned home, I went straight to bed. The next morning, my aunt saw the blood. I heard her telling Mama that I was a young lady. Mama came into the room and helped me to clean up. She made a bag out of brown cotton material and about a dozen square pieces of the same material she called napkins. She tied a string around my waist and showed me how to fold and attach the napkin to my body. She told me I must change and wash them every morning and evening and keep them clean. During her demonstration, she said, "Do not let no little boy put his killy (Willy) there," as she pointed to my private area. I was so confused and embarrassed; I had no idea what she was talking about.

When she left the room, I was even more traumatized, frightened, and confused. I did not know or understand what was going on with my body. "Why was I bleeding? Is it going to stop?" I got no explanation, no information, and no reassurance that everything would be all right. I sat there and stared at the walls. I became voiceless and immovable and deaf since I couldn't even hear my name when Mama called me. Sometime later, Mama peeked in the room and asked me if I did not hear her calling me. I said nothing. I came outside and saw my breakfast on the table. I gobbled down everything so quickly. I can't remember if I said, "thank you" or prayed before I ate. It had been one day since I had eaten.

After a few days, the bleeding stopped. I felt so relieved. A significant burden had been lifted, allowing me to concentrate on my schoolwork. During this time, I had to go to school. Mama told me I could not stay at home. This horrifying experience happened a few months before my eleventh birthday. Imagine my surprise when the same thing happened again after a few weeks. I was left wondering why it happened again! That summer (we also called summer "August Holiday"), I went to Uncle Urban and Aunty Carmen. I did not know I had to take my napkins bag with me, so I left them behind. To my surprise, it happened again. This time, Aunty Carmen saw it. She explained everything to me. I finally got the talk about "The Birds and the Bees." She gave me disposable pads and told me not to flush them down the toilet. There were no outhouses here. She showed me how to dispose of them properly. I felt relieved. I understood that this was a natural part of becoming a woman. When I was leaving, Aunty Carmen gave me three packs of pads to last a few months and money to purchase more when they ran out. Well Ingrid, welcome to puberty and the mysterious wonder of the changing body of a young lady.

I wondered what the mystery surrounding this process was. Why did Mama not explain everything? She told me everything else, or so I thought. It's part of the natural process of womanhood. She told me about her life with her parents, stories about her marriage to my grandfather, and why she left him, about working in Watooka as a maid, even her dancing and winning trophies as a young lady. She even told me she got pregnant after she left Dada, but she cast it away (had an abortion) because she did not want to have different children. But she never told me or prepared me for puberty, even when it happened. I have a deficit on words for this one, so I will move on to what I can understand and explain.

I joined the Lions Club and took part in many of their activities. There were only girls in this club, so we were called Lionesses. We practiced many drills and floor exercises while the police band played. We were the highlight of many events in the town. We also traveled out of town on many occasions to display our talents. I took part in Lions Club activities for about two years before my passionate preparation for the adult world began.

My grandmother had a tight grip on me. I could not go to parties or even the cinema or visit friends unless she knew their parents. Mama only allowed me to go to church. I joined the Assemblies of God Church. There was a youth meeting called The Christ Ambassadors or CA every Sunday afternoon. I only wanted to attend these meetings to get out of the house. Also, young people conducted the services. I was not allowed to go alone. Mama trusted Brother Innocent (we called him Innar), a much older, prominent and trustworthy church member. He invited me to church, and Mama said that I could go. However, Brother Innocent was commissioned to take me to and from the church every Sunday afternoon and on special occasions. He considered this a pleasure as he took this responsibility seriously. He was always happy and smiling and seemed to have a chip in his walk.

Sunday afternoons had now become very important. I had ulterior motives. I asked my friends to keep their parties and get-togethers on Sunday afternoons between 6 and 8:30. So I could slip away from CA, make it to the party and be back before the evening church service was over. Sometimes I just left for the hell of it, just to hang out with my friends. Boyfriends were not involved. Just three or four girls together in Kelly's home "shooting breeze," talking about boys or the latest news in the town. Kelly lived with her aunt who was a housewife. She was very accommodating to us. She fed us well and even joined in our conversation. I loved going to Kelly's house on Sundays. Her aunt was always throwing out nuggets of wisdom. I remember vividly as if it were yesterday, she told us never to listen when a boy tells us that if we loved him, we would have sex with him. She said to run in the opposite direction because he would leave us and find another girlfriend when we get pregnant. She told us if we were being pressured to have sex, run away. She told us never to go anywhere with a boy alone because it will lead to sex. She also told us that young men only have sex on their minds. She told us many more stories about boys. I took what she said seriously. Even though I did not know the circumstances of my conception, I knew my mother became pregnant by a man who did not love her and may have told her the same things. He left my mother when she became pregnant. I did not want to suffer the same faith.

Mama was never aware of my Sunday afternoon nefarious activities and no one told her. Anyway, can you see how I had perfected the art of the "sneaky craft" I learned from my cousins? It came full circle. Sometimes I almost got caught; I always had a very good "story to tell." A few times Brother Innocent said, "I did not see you in CA." I said, convincingly, "I was there, where else could I be?" Or, "I was in another seat at the back of the church." The church was always full. I thought perhaps, with my little "smart" self, that he could not know the difference. Or maybe he suspected that I slipped out and did not want to let me know. Whatever the case was, I had fun, and I got away with it, or so I thought.

One Sunday afternoon, my craftiness did not work out. Innar sat next to me and I just could not escape, so I pretended to be sick at the beginning of CA. I thought this was the right time so I could leave by myself. Innar said, "I will take you home." I felt squished like the little bug I was. I can now laugh at this incident, but back then, I was as "mad as hell." After about thirty plus years, I went home on vacation, saw Innar and he reminded me about this incident and how he got into trouble because the church did not allow men to transport young ladies on their bicycles. What an antiquated law! I apologized to him because he got into trouble, but I did not tell him I was not really sick in the first place. I left that for another time and season. I did not want to embarrass myself in the presence of my nieces and nephew. I guess they will know now! I wonder what else I had done that he did not mention!

Mama had such a tight grip on me she did not want to let me out of her sight. She took me to work anytime I would be alone at home during the day. One day as I was sitting on the steps reading, one of the young men, her boss's son came down the stairs, grabbed my book out of my hand, threw it away, forced me to lie down on the steps, and got on top of me. My young instincts kicked in, and I caught him on his breast and bit him as hard as I could. He jumped up and I kicked him in the groin. He collided on the side of the lattice stairway. I jumped up and ran to Mama who was cooking in the kitchen. She must have seen the terrified look on my face and asked me what happened. I said nothing. I kept staring at the wall, with my heart pounding and hands and feet trembling. I felt as though I was in a different world.

Once again, I was voiceless. Mama did not insist for an answer, she kept on cooking. I retrieved my book several hours later before we went home. Later I told Mama I did not want to go back there. She said that I would have to remain in the house and not go outside to play. We made this agreement and it worked for me.

Mama encouraged me and taught me responsibility in her own way. I was about thirteen years old when one weekend when Uncle Andy came to visit, Mama told me to cook. When I asked her what to cook, she said, "Cook anything." I looked around the kitchen and found fried snapper, rice, chow mein noodles, potatoes, and other vegetables, meat, bora (long bean) and seasoning. I could not cook stewed fish or bora because there was no tomato paste or tomatoes. I could not use the meat because Mama had to make soup the following day which was Sunday. I decided on the next best thing. I chopped up the fish and bora, boiled and strained the noodles, Seasoned the bora and fish, and cooked them together. I made a delicious fish chow mein. When Uncle Andy saw the dish, he shook his head and said, "My niece, the domestic science student made fish chow mein." He sat down with Mama and ate. They even asked for seconds. I stood there in silence with a smile on my face and watched them eat this delicious meal without laughing or criticizing me. When my aunt came home and saw her dinner, she laughed and said loudly, "Who cook fish chow Mein? Fish don't go with chow mein. Wha kinda thing is this?" No one answered, we just looked at her. She dished out some food, tasted it and said, "it ain't taste bad." I think Mama and Uncle Andy did not laugh because they did not want to hurt my feelings. I guess this was "one for the ages." I never cooked fish chow mein again. Now, I can laugh at myself!

My grandmother and I did lots of things together. We went on many one-day bus trips to unfamiliar parts of the country. We went to many dances. Even though she was an accomplished dancer, I have never seen her dancing. She said when she was young, she won many prizes in dancing competitions. Whenever she went to dances with me, she always worked in the kitchen serving or cooking food. Our parties and dances always had cooked food such as cook-up-rice, chow mein, curry, and roti and snacks, such as souse, patties, cheese rolls, pine tarts, and cakes. I am not sure what the difference between a dance and a party is. The food is free at a party, whereas at a dance, it is for fundraising purposes; so, the food, snacks, and drinks, including liquor, are sold. When Mama organized her

Self-Help Housing Scheme, the group kept many dances to raise funds for their down payment.

Saturdays seemed to be special days of hard manual labor. There were housecleaning, laundry, marketing, and baking. In fact, it began on Fridays, when Mama gave me the grocery list to take to "Doctor Shop" (a grocery store) to pick up the groceries after school. After a while, she made me check the safe (cupboard) to see what we needed, and then I had to write the grocery list and take it to the shop. She stopped and paid for the groceries on her way home after she left work. Early on Saturday mornings, she gave me a market list and money to go to the market. After a while, she stopped writing the market list and gave me the money to go to the market. She said, "Buy what the house needs." I guess this was her crude way of teaching me responsibility, a lesson I have learned well, and one that benefited me later in life. She used to give the money to my aunt to go to the market. However, this did not work out. She never bought enough food, did not return the change and by the middle of the week we did not have any food in the house. Mama had to use the little change she had to buy more food. There was always an argument at this time because Mama believed she put the money to her own use.

There were no washing machines and dryers. We used a tub or basin with a scrubbing board to wash our clothes, and then they were dried on the clothesline. May God help us if it rained that day! It meant that the wet clothes had to be picked up and placed in a basket and hung out to dry the following day. Sometimes, they were hung out to dry in the house if it seemed that it would rain the next day.

The floors, including the kitchen, living room and bedroom had to be swept and washed, including the stairs, both front and back. We did not have mops and vacuum cleaners. I had to get down on my hands and knees and scrape the kitchen floors and stairs, using a bucket, scraper, and floor cloth. The living room had to be wiped, polished and shined. There were no gloves to protect my hands or knee pads to protect my knees.

Mama taught me how to cook and bake. I also learned these techniques in my home economics classes in school. We did not have a stove, so we cooked in a fireside or a coal pot. Later, Uncle Andy bought a one-burner then a two-burner kerosene oil stove. We did not have a refrigerator. This made it difficult for us to store fresh fruits, meat and vegetables for more than a day or two. Meat and fish had to be cooked the same day when they were bought. We bought ice daily and kept them in an insulated ice bucket.

Mama raised chickens in a coop under the house. We kept our eggs in an open bowl and turned them every day to prevent them from spoiling. We left some in the coop for the chickens to hatch. The eggs were eaten or sold quickly, anyway. We did not have a toaster, so we used a frying pan or a tawa (a flat pan with one handle) to toast our bread.

We did not have a television or stereo set. All we had was an old radio, which Mama turned on every night to listen to the news and death announcements or obituaries when she was at home. We kept informed of local and world news by listening to the radio and reading the Guyana Chronicle Newspapers. The radio was also our prime source of entertainment at home as we listened to music and stories created by our local artists.

Mama made the best loaves of bread, cakes and pastries. I enjoyed working with her in our tiny kitchen. When we were finished mixing and putting the dough into pans, we took them to the "baker shop" (Bakery) since we did not have a large oven at home. We had a little mud oven next to the fireside. The "baker shop" was often crowded, and we had to wait on our turn for the baker to put our bakery goods in the large brick oven. This was our routine every Saturday afternoon. I loved having hot bread and butter for dinner on Saturday nights. On Sunday mornings, we had fresh bread with fried or scrambled eggs and sometimes with bacon or ham. Sometimes we had a stew with fish or sardines or salted fish (codfish). On special occasions such as Christmas or Easter, we had Pepper Pot. This was a dish prepared with cassareep (a dark brown sweet sauce made from cassava or yuca root) with meat including beef, pork, tripe, cow heel, and pig feet. Pepper Pot was delicious. This dish is also the native dish of the Amerindians who are the aborigines or original people in Guyana. The African and other races in Guyana adopted Pepper Pot from the Amerindians.

Also, every Sunday, Mama cooked soup without fail. The soup was like a religion on Sundays—it had to be present. There was a split pea, black eye peas, callaloo (spinach), fish head, eddo, just about anything. She made a soup with almost any peas or vegetable. Fufu was always on the menu. This was made by pounding boiled green plantains with a mortar and pestle and formed into balls.

On some Sunday afternoons, Mama made ice cream from scratch. Then, we churned the custard in an ice cream can by hand. It was hard work, but we loved having ice cream with cakes or pastries including patties, cheese rolls, and pine tarts. We also made different types of sweet bread and cakes. She sometimes bought bread and cakes during the week when we ran out of our homemade goodies. We also made different types of fried bakes—soft, cornmeal or just plain. Sometimes, when my grandmother was at work, my aunt would do the baking. I would die to get Mama's raisin-cinnamon bread and rolls and also her sweetbreads now. They were so good! Mama also made different types of drinks, including Jamun and rice wines, mauby, five fingers (star fruit), sorrel, bellembee (lady finger or sourie), lime, lemon, passion fruit, tamarind and many more. If there was a fruit in Guyana, my grandmother could make a drink or wine out of it. She did everything without using a recipe book.

I wish I had taken notes instead of trying to be a magician in the kitchen now. Spending time with my grandmother was precious; I would not exchange it for anything else in this world. I'll forever be grateful for the precious, wonderful and now memorable times we spent together in the kitchen.

Life was not always great for us. Sometimes food and money were scarce. I stood alongside Mama when she rummaged through the garbage cans in the market to find the "good food" while I held the bag for her to put them in. She took greens and vegetables, no fish or meat. Many times, when I saw my friends during this retrieval event, I would hide behind Mama in embarrassment and for fear that my friends would laugh or tease me in school. She took the food home, washed and cooked it; we ate it, we were well-nourished and lived many years later to tell this tale.

Mama heard the news on the radio and she also read in the newspapers that low-income houses were being built in Georgetown our capital. She then conceived the idea that those same houses could be built in New Amsterdam too. She thought if she could put together a group of ambitious people willing to put forward their efforts and time, they could build and own homes. This was a herculean task since the people had to be convinced that this was an achievable and worthwhile project. They had never heard or seen anything like this in our town. So, while she was organizing a group, she was also trying to contact different Ministers of the Government to find out who was in the best position to help her. While I was in primary school, I helped Mama type letters to several government officials including the President of Guyana who was the Honorable L.F.S Burnham.

Mama discussed her plans with her friends and others in the neighborhood and just about anyone she thought would enjoy living in a better environment or who would listen to her. She was relentless in her recruitment efforts. They held several meetings to plan and strategize and to raise funds for the down-payment. Initially, the meetings were held in our tiny house in "Jill yard"–the ghetto. After they identified the building site, they held their meetings there. The crowd became too big to fit in our tiny house. During this project's planning phase, many people had dropped out, especially when they learned that money was involved. Mama had a notebook with a lengthy list of names of about forty potential homeowners. When they became disinterested, she crossed their names out. Anyway, Mama kept on working with those who were interested. Many of them accused her of taking their money and many people did not believe they could achieve homeownership. However, Mama took no one's money and converted it to her own cause. She opened a bank account and deposited all the money she collected. The group members gave money for their down payment according to their means. I cannot remember how much the down payment was. Also, the group elected a president, secretary, and treasurer and committee members who were accountable and were given the task of overseeing the day-to-day operations of the group's project.

Mama always took me to Georgetown whenever she had to visit various Ministers in the Government. She always went without an appointment and demanded to see whichever Minister she thought would assist her cause to build self-help houses in her community. On one occasion she went to the office of the President of Guyana without an appointment and demanded to see him, and she did. She never left an office until she got an answer that satisfied her. This lady was bold and determined and a force to reckon with. I typed all of her letters and kept carbon copies for her records. So, when she approached a Minister, she had all of her evidence. Sometimes she did not get replies to her letters. I remember when she went to see the Minister of Housing; she showed the secretary her copy and asked her if she threw the letter in there, as she pointed to the wastebasket.

Whenever we went to Georgetown, we never spent the night. We caught the first boat out of New Amsterdam and spent the entire day. Mama bought no food. She said she worked in restaurants and knew what they did and how the food was prepared, so she took food and homemade drinks for us. We dined at any convenient spot—the park benches, stairways, or just about any place that was strong enough to support us. Our dining experience needed no reservations or special places of comfort. The food was always cold, having been prepared the night before.

Mama made several presentations to the government to build self-help houses. Since she did not know which Ministry was responsible for building these houses, she kept on inquiring until she reached the President's office. He pointed her in the right direction. Meanwhile, my aunt kept telling her that she was wasting her time, and no one would give her a house. Mama did what she always did, rolled her eyes and hissed her teeth. Then one day, I think she was sick and tired of hearing the same nonsense. She said to my aunt in a harsh tone, "Shut yo damn mouth." With hands-on her hips, she stood there and looked at my aunt as though she was ready to go into battle. My aunt looked at Mama and said nothing. This ended the negative innuendoes.

After about three to four years of searching, enquiring, and planning, the project finally came to fruition. The building plans were approved, and the buildings were now under construction. The government sent supervisors to make sure that the houses were being built according to specifications. Incidentally, my aunt became the secretary and was hired to manage the clerical part of the construction. This included record-keeping of materials and timesheets of all workers and financial records. Every day the members came to the construction site after work or whenever they found the time during the day or night to build their own homes. The group members consisted of both men and women who worked very hard to build their houses. Some even worked into the wee hours of the morning and all day on Saturdays and Sundays. When some unbelievers saw that the housing project was becoming a reality, they wanted to rejoin the group. Mama said, "No, you are doubting Thomas, too late now." She said it without any conviction or empathy.

Everyone had a specific amount of time to work on the houses. The houses were built collectively. No one knew which house they would get until they built all the houses. After construction, the members drew numbers from a bag. Mama had the privilege to choose which house she wanted. I guess it's because she was the founder. She chose the first house. The members built twenty-five houses. This was the first self-help housing scheme in the region. It was called "Pearl Stewart Housing Scheme" after my grandmother. Later, other housing schemes were built in that area. Sometimes it only takes one resilient person to make a difference.

If I knew anything about my grandmother, I knew she was determined to get what she wanted. We were now set to move out of the ghetto and into a brand new two-bedroom house. Since we were moving, this was one less thing I had to worry about. By the time I was ready to leave high school, my grandmother already had an organized and functional "Self-Help Group" working together to build low-income houses.

I remembered several years earlier Uncle Andy telling Mama that she should move out of the ghetto into a larger and more convenient house and that he would pay the rent. She said to him, "When I leave 'Jill yard,' I am going into my own house." The family wanted to know what she was talking about. No one knew how she would achieve this feat without having adequate funds to purchase her own home. Everyone thought she would return to the Corentyne to build a little house on the parcel of land she inherited from her parents. For several years, Uncle Andy made the same request for her to move. Every time, she gave him the same response. Mama did not budge; she was very strong and resilient. She said it, and it became a reality. Now the Pearl Stewart Housing Scheme still stands. Mama's dream of homeownership became a reality. Many of the residents renovated their homes because of growing family needs. Some have remained the same, and some have fallen to neglect. However, my grandmother's legacy still lives on. Later, when I went to work in the Caribbean, I paid off the mortgage for this house.

When my grandmother moved into her own home, Uncle Andy bought a new refrigerator and a gas stove with an oven and new furniture. Even though there was an oven in the house, Uncle Andy made her a box oven under the house that was larger than the gas oven. We used the box oven more because we could bake more bread and cakes in one batch and be finished in less time.

It may appear as though we were deprived, and we were, but we were happy together. My grandmother and I shared a special and cohesive bond. However, there was always an aura of genuine love and contentment mingled with hope and promise of a brighter future. It's hard to explain the complexities of my childhood and then to understand when one has not gone through the pain and agony of life in the ghetto.

As an adult, when I look back, Mama exposed me to various lifestyles. I knew she wanted me to raise my standard of life, to have a fuller and more rewarding lifestyle when I became an adult. Thank God for giving her the insight to remove me from my mother's house and molding me into an untraditional and successful woman.

Natasha (my aunt's daughter) and me.
My Grandmother's house is in the background. This is one of the houses in the Pearl Stewart Housing Scheme- named after my grandmother. I made my dress and handbag, as well as Natasha's dress.

Mama relaxing in her backyard.
Under one of the many fruit trees she planted.

Some Equipment in Mama's Home

We did not have much. Mama used what she had and never complained.
She often used the expression,
"You cannot fly in the face of God because you don't have what you want." We were never hungry or desolate.
Mama seemed to make a little go a long way.

Laundry and Cleaning Days

"Days of agony and torture; yet this necessity was paramount in keeping our home and clothing clean and tidy."

A Pointer Broom

Made from the main vein of the coconut tree leaf. Several of these veins were stripped and put together and tied in a bundle using pieces of rags from old clothes. As children, we made these brooms when dry branches fell from the coconut trees. It took several branches to make one broom. The green branches were seldom used to make brooms.

This broom was used to sweep the house and yard. Sometimes, these pointers were used to make kites.

A scrubbing (washing) board. Was placed in the tub to scrub clothes.

A galvanized tub used for washing clothes, bathing & storing water.

Laundry day was usually on Saturdays. However, sometimes laundry was done during the week. Our underwear had to be washed every day and hung out to dry in the house. On Friday evenings, the clothes were soaked in the tub with soap or soap powder and left in the kitchen. Then, they were washed, rinsed, wrung and hung out to dry on clothes lines. Clothes pins kept the clothes from falling as they swayed in the wind.

Sometimes, starch was placed on the clothes after the rinse "cycle." Starch was made by placing boiling water on the dry white starch and stirring it. My aunt insisted that the starch had to be mixed to a certain consistency – not too thick and not too thin. My aunt always insisted that the clothes must be rinsed twice before hanging them out. Once was not enough. The tub was also used to store water for bathing, washing dishes and clothes and also the house.

A Calabash

Used for dipping water

A Galvanized Bucket

Used to fetch and store water especially when taking a bath.

A Flat Iron

Most of our ironing was done on Saturdays or Sunday afternoons. This iron was used for ironing clothes. They were placed on the coal pot or fireside to be heated. They were wiped clean with a cloth before ironing clothes. Since iron tends to rust, when we were finished ironing, we rubbed them with beef suet while they were warm to preserve them. A cloth was wrapped around the handle to prevent our hands from burning. Before ironing, we sprinkled the clothes lightly with water to make them smooth while ironing.

Another type of iron was the charcoal iron. The coal was placed inside the iron and lighted. When the iron was hot, it could be used for ironing. Beef suet was also used to preserve this iron. This iron made perfect pleats on my uniforms. We had our own way of steaming while using this iron. A wet cotton cloth was placed over the pleats, and then you ran the hot iron over until the cloth was dry. The pleats were kept perfectly straight and razor sharp even when my uniforms were washed. After washing, my uniforms were not rung or squeezed, they were hung out to dry (drip dry) so that the pleats were kept straight and smooth.

Lighting

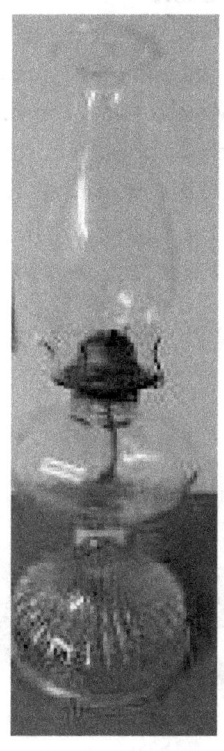

Kerosene oil Lamps

Lamps were a necessary convenience for the dark.

Mama never used candles or battery lamps. Over the years, we changed many lamps. The shades were either cracked or were accidentally broken. I used lamps to study and do my homework whenever I woke up early in the mornings. Our home always had at least three lamps. Sometimes they were hung on the wall, placed on the table, or hung from the rafters. The lamp shades often got black with soot as the wick burned and had to be washed and dried during the day.

All of our lamps used kerosene oil. It was my job to buy the "kero oil" as it was called. "The kero oil" was stored in special cans. This oil was also used as a starter for the fireside and the coal pot. All of the lamps were turned off before we went to bed at night. We used kerosene lamps sometimes at night when Mama wanted to save money on electricity.

Cooking and Baking Equipment

Mama made delicious entrees. Sometimes we took our bread and pastries to bake in the baker shop (bakery). We also had a mud oven next to our fireside. This oven was used whenever we could not go to the baker shop, or when Mama baked late at nights. This mud oven was also convenient, because Mama baked her pastries in it whenever she had to cater for an event.

The Coal Pot

Coal was placed inside the coal pot. It was used for cooking and baking. The coal pot was also placed inside the box oven when baking.

The Tawa with Roti

Used to bake roti, dahl pouri/puri, bakes and cassava bread.

Triumphs of a Little Girl

A Patty Pan with patties

*Used for making patties. Mama's
pans had six holes instead of twelve.*

A half coconut and old grater

*The coconut was cut in half. The serrated edge
was used to strip/grate the coconut.
It's easier to sit on the handle and rub the coconut on the serrated edge.
There were other graters as well, many of them homemade.*

As children, we made our graters from tin-cans. We cut the cans in half with a pair of sheers, then we used nails and a hammer to make several holes covering the entire surface. Our homemade graters were a useful invention but dangerous. We got hurt many times trying to grate coconuts. However, we persisted because our bush cook was special.

My Cultural Heritage

Guyanese culture is an assimilation of the races in our country. Each race is a part of a sub-culture with its own beliefs, arts, customs, and religious observances. Unique in its ways, each social group presents a special touch that makes Guyana a true "melting pot."

Guyana is included in the Caribbean because our culture and socio-economic status is similar in many ways.

I was born in Guyana of African descent. I guess when the African slaves were brought to British Guiana, they came with their cultural heritage and customs. They passed this down from generation to generation by word of mouth. In such transitions, they have lost many of the fundamental features because of slavery, time, and modernization. We now have the remnants of what it used to be somewhere on the African continent.

There is good and evil in every culture. As a child, growing up in Guyana, I had a first-class ticket in the arena of good and evil. Most of the phenomena were unexplainable, and some would leave you asking, "How did that happen?" and with a puzzled look on your face for days or years. Other instances would leave you wondering, "Why did they do that?" We observed what was happening and went about our daily lives hoping that the incident would never happen to us.

My culture has its roots in the combination of African, East Indians, Chinese, Caucasian, and Amerindian. The food, holidays and other social factors prove the essence of each subculture. The various subcultures come together during holidays such as Christmas, Easter and Mashramani. However, I identify as a descendant from African parentage.

Ghana Day Celebration

This was a special day in August. Perhaps the slaves in my region came from Ghana. There was folk music and dancing in the streets. They served food and drinks after the frolicking was over. I think this holiday was only celebrated once.

Obeah and Superstition

My neighbor, Mr. Felix, invited the neighborhood children a few times a year and fed us well. He gave us curried chicken with white rice, cakes, and drinks. There were many stipulations while we ate this delicious meal. We could not chew the bones or throw away the leftover food in the garbage. We couldn't even take food away. Everything had to be eaten in his house. Later in the evening, I heard a brief noise outside, so I peered through the crease in the wall of our house as I usually did. I saw Mr. Felix digging a hole in the ground at his front steps. He buried the bones and leftover food and then covered the hole. Meanwhile, before they cooked the food, he bought a live white chicken, killed it, then drained and buried the blood under his steps, plucked the feathers, and prepared it for cooking. This was the same chicken we ate at the party.

Even though we could not play outside when Mama was not at home, I peeped through the many creases in the walls and windows of our little wooden house and saw the entire "goings on" in our yard. The first time I saw Mr. Felix's "party preparation," I wondered what the significance was and asked Mama about it. She said, "Felix is too damn superstitious. He wants to keep his job." Later, I heard Mama saying that when children are fed, it brings good luck to the person who provided the food. Now, I wondered about this! Let me think, "So, you killed a chicken, drained and buried the blood under the steps, cooked the chicken, gave a party for children, buried the bones and leftover food, and you get to keep your job?" This is very interesting and mind-boggling. I do not know how much good luck this was. He was living in the ghetto with the rest of us. The only difference was that his house had a bathroom and running water. We all shared the same latrine and were subjected to the same awful ghetto living conditions. What about you, Mr. Felix, doing your work efficiently and trust in God for a promotion? I wondered how this worked for him. He was in the same position on his job two years later.

Maria was about five years old, when one afternoon after school, as I was approaching my home, I saw a crowd standing on the street looking into our yard. As I got closer, I heard a loud voice screaming, "Awe Mammy, Awe Mammy, Awe Mammy." When I looked, I saw Maria hanging out of her window. Her eyes were white while she stretched her tongue out of her mouth about six inches. She kept on screaming, attracting everyone, while her mom and two other adults tried hard to hold her and prevent her from jumping through the window. Maria, about five years old, seemed to have superhuman strength. About an hour later, I saw a man going into the house. I do not know what he did, but they got Maria from the window, and the screaming stopped. When I saw Maria the following day, she seemed normal. Later I heard Mama telling my aunt that Maria's mom left her husband and hooked up with her old 'sweetheart', who was the father of her sister's children. They were all separated and had their own families at this time. After several years, the younger sister left her husband and rekindled the love affair with her old lover, who was now married to another woman. The two sisters and his wife were now at war. The wife left the marriage. The two sisters were now at war between themselves. One decided to get rid of the other by sending spirits to kill or injure the other. The spirits held on to Maria instead of her mother, who was their original assignment. Maria's mom told her friends he was her man first. Her sister took him away from her when they were young, and now she was taking him back. She boasted flamboyantly that, "No obeah can catch me. I will send it back." I do not know what happened, but I never saw this Casanova visiting the home again. Also, his kids and I attended the same elementary school. After a while, they disappeared. I never saw nor heard from them again. I believe they left town.

My next paranormal event was during the lunch period. As we were getting out of school to go home, we noticed an enormous crowd on Main Street. As we drew closer, we noticed that stones were being thrown at a sizeable house. The only problem was, no one knew or saw where the stones were coming from. Some people made this a lunchtime entertainment event and laughed. They were then stoned as well, and no one saw who was throwing the stones or what direction they were coming from. Most of the crowd dispersed immediately after they were stoned. This continued for the rest of the day, through the night and a few days later. I heard the adults say that the landlord wanted to repossess his property, and the occupants did not want to vacate the premises. So, the landlord went to a town in Suriname (a neighboring country known for its rich demonic practices) to get "something" to get them out. That resulted from an unknown entity scaring his tenants into leaving his property. What do you know? They all left. Later, I heard another story. The landlord rented the house to one woman. She sublet the rooms to other people and was making a huge profit from this business. When the landlord heard about this nefarious activity, he gave her notice to vacate the premises. She and her tenants did not want to leave. So, his solution was to scare them. The spirits hurt no one during this melee. When the tenants moved out, the stoning ended. There was peace again on Main Street. But, as children, whenever we passed the house, we always looked around to see if we could see "something," perhaps the "jumbee" or ghost that was throwing the stones. Maybe they were returned to the sender. We never saw anything.

We lived next to an Indian family. I am not sure if they were Muslims or Hindus or another religion. Anyway, the oldest daughter was going overseas to study. Her parents held a ceremony in her honor. They invited my sister and me, but Mama told us not to go. So, I did what I always did, peeped through the creases in the walls and windows. I noticed that they placed her hands over the fire while they recited something in another language. Her hands were not burned. I later learned that they intended this ritual to bring her success in her studies abroad.

During one of my Sunday night visits to church, a young lady came into the church and crawled under the pews on her hands and knees. As she crawled, her eyes were closed, but somehow, she knew how to navigate from pew to pew without obstruction. The singing stopped, and the pastor led the church in prayer. The ushers got hold of her and took her to the altar for prayer. The pastor placed his hands on her forehead and casted the demons out. She screamed and trembled and she fell on the ground in silence. I do not know what happened, but she was still on the ground when the service was over. Later, I learned that someone did "something" to her because she was smart in school. That person did not want her to succeed.

This next incident came close to home. Sometime after I left high school, I went to live with my mother in Linden. Every Sunday night after church, Owen, Lennox and I walked home together. Then, we stood under the streetlights around the circle and talked and debated just about any topic. When we were finished, they took me home, and then they went home. We all lived near to each other. One Sunday night, as we stood talking, as usual, Lennox said, "Look, Miss Marie." When we turned around, we saw Miss Marie sitting on her back step as she usually did. We scampered toward our homes. As I was running upstairs, I saw a pair of the largest eyes I have ever seen looking up at me. The stairs never seemed so long until that night. You may ask why we ran. Miss Marie recently passed away, and here we were seeing her, as usual, sitting on her back steps. When we saw each other on Monday morning, we laughed until it hurt. We never congregated under those streetlights again.

Some people are so superstitious, and it's just not funny. One day I went across the street to visit my friend Desiree. I saw an Obeah man leaving with one of my cousins. When they were clearly out of sight, Ms. Vee, Desiree's mom, said she was waiting on this Obeah man to give her a portion because her mom was sick and they did not know what happened to her. Ms. Vee said while she was waiting on him in the living room, this man was in the kitchen mixing and grinding coals and ash from the coal pot, and then he added some of her pink face powder. He gave my cousin this mixture and told her to rub it on her mother's skin and she will get better. In exchange, she gave him some money. When Mama came home that night, I told her what happened. Mama rolled her eyes, hissed her teeth and said in a harsh tone, "They too damn superstitious. Them should take Mazie to a doctor if they want to know what happened to her."

Whenever I visited my cousins, I noticed that they had a broom over the door and a glass of water next to Cousin Mazie's bed. They believed the broom prevented evil spirits from entering the house, and a glass of water absorbed evil influences. There were also lighted white candles burning on the nightstand with an open Bible next to her bed. I do not know what the significance of this was. Cousin Mazie continued to cry and roll from side to side in pain and agony. This continued for about four months until one day, she died. The postmortem (autopsy) revealed that she had uterine cancer that metastasized and spread to other organs. Maybe, her life could have been saved, or she could have lived longer if a doctor had seen her and she was given the proper treatment. That family believed all along that somebody did something evil to Cousin Mazie. It's too bad that some of us would allow our beliefs and superstition to ruin our lives.

In some families, superstition is the norm. Some examples are: "Do not cross your feet when you sit, because you will have bad luck." "Do not put your hat on the bed, it will bring you misfortune." "Do not pay your debts at night, because it will bring you misfortune." "When you wash your hands do not wring them out because you cannot keep money," and many, many more. The do's and don'ts were too many to mention. I was very inquisitive as a child. Whenever I heard something strange, I asked Mama about it. Sometimes, she explained and other times she would say, "Don't ask me no damn stupidness." Mama never indulged in superstitions. She never believed in intangibles. If you could not give her hard evidence, she would not even entertain the thought.

Sometimes I thought she was strange because she did not believe in strange phenomena. There were churches that indulged in questionable religious practices in the name of God. They claimed to be healers while practicing witchcraft. My aunt usually got a delightful laugh whenever she talked about these healers. She said, "Dem tek out wan and put in dee other." Meaning, that they removed one demon and put in another demon. Later, as I got older, Uncle Andy knew I was very curious, so he told me not to get involved in the occult because I could get seriously hurt. Many people who were practicing witchcraft did not know what they were doing. In Guyana, Africans have lost some factual information and procedures about their culture since they were passed down from generation to generation through word of mouth. Each generation has become "more modern" or has turned to Christianity and, therefore, has turned away and lost their cultural identity. Always trust in God; that's the only correct way to go. So, I stopped all inquiries into the unexplainable. I did not like getting hurt. There are so many crazy stories I can tell that was evident in my community. I couldn't make this stuff up.

Christmas Celebrations

I now turn my attention to another part of my culture; One that is happy, not confusing, and easily explainable. During the Christmas season, like in many countries around the world, we celebrated the birth of Jesus. It was a time to spread joy, receive and give gifts, and eat special foods such as black cake, pepper pot, souse, aniseed bread, and garlic pork. Mama also made sorrel drink, mauby, and ginger beer, and sometimes rice or jamun wine. We didn't have much, but somehow at Christmas, it appeared it was a feast. Every home was "broken down," or we rearranged the furniture several weeks in advance. By Christmas Eve, the homes would be cleaned and redecorated with new curtains and sometimes new furniture. Most people put up new curtains on Christmas Eve night so that on Christmas morning when they flung open their windows, they could show off their new curtains and take a peek at other people's curtains and even evaluated curtains in the neighborhood. Everyone seemed so happy as they shared Christmas cheers. My Uncle Andy and friends came over to Mama's house and she fed them.

As children, we always expected toys at Christmas. This was the only time we got toys. Uncle Andy always gave us toys. A few times, he hid the gifts and gave us on Christmas morning, then lied to us and said Santa Claus left them for us. I always knew of this trick that adults played. I knew Santa Claus was not real, even though Mama or my aunt took us to see him during the Christmas Holidays. Somehow, when I saw him on Christmas cards, he was always a big fat white guy. But, when I saw him in person, he was always black with a fake white beard. They told me that this was Black Santa. Then when we went to another store and saw a fat white man who was also Santa. I guess this was the adults' way of keeping this fallacy and our innocence alive. Another thing we were told was that Santa came down the chimney to bring toys for the good children. We did not have a chimney. So, if Santa liked to come down into our fireside, he would have to remove our zinc sheets over the fireside and come on in. He and our toys would be burned anyway. It would be easier for him just to leave our gifts on the veranda or back steps. If he had knocked on the door, Mama would have invited him in and gave him some ginger beer, black cake and pastries. If the pepperpot was finished, she would have given him some too. Further, since he only gave good children gifts, he could have saved himself a trip because we were not very good children anyway. Oh well!

The other event when I got gifts sometimes was on my birthday. They gave me books. Mama made my favorite three-color-cake. As usual, I did not get a birthday party. I remember asking for a party once. When July 15th came around, Mama took the day off from her work. She made my usual favorite three-color-cake, with pastries, homemade drinks, food, chow mien, roti, and curry. The cake was not decorated with icing, but we placed ten little candles on top of the cake. I made a new dress for the occasion. I invited my two friends who Mama approved. We had a good time eating and talking. Mama turned on the radio so we could dance to music on the air. This is how I spent my tenth birthday. I never asked for another birthday party again. Lesson learned; we could not afford to have a birthday party. I was not sad about it, because I knew when I grew up, I would have lavish parties, or so I thought. This never happened. I attended many birthday parties, but I never gave myself one. I do not know why. Perhaps I was just too busy working, studying, or I may have lost interest. Time goes by when we are not paying attention. Sometimes, we tend to neglect ourselves while we take care of others. My life has been a combination of all the above. I may correct this and have a party at some point. Wish me luck!

Back to our Christmas holiday celebrations, I liked the Masquerade band. This band had its origin in slavery and was passed down through the generations. They made two appearances during the year, one at Christmas and the other during the Mashramani celebrations in February each year.

They dressed the band members in colorful clothing. They danced, played music on their drums and sang folk songs as they marched or tramped through the streets. Everyone admired them and sometimes joined in the fun. They were given food, drinks, and money along the way. I looked forward to seeing the "long lady." I often wondered how she could walk on stilts attached to her feet. As a child, I remembered this as the tallest lady I had ever seen. She wore a long flowing skirt that covered the stilts. The stilts were not visible. As she walked, she danced to the music, and her beautiful skirt moved with the rhythm. This was a beautiful sight.

During the Christmas holidays, the markets were filled with the welcome sight of grapes and apples. These were imported fruits that appeared only at Christmas. The apples were called iced apples. I do not know the origin of this name, but they were delicious and a welcome change from the usual fruits we ate during the year.

Kite Flying on Easter Monday

Kite flying was and still is a tradition on Easter Monday. Sometimes, one of the neighborhood kids would allow me to fly his/her kite for a few minutes. Mama could not always afford to buy us kites for Easter Monday. It was fun watching the kites as they flew in the bright Easter Monday sky. Somehow, most Easter Mondays always seemed to be dry and bright, no rain or gray clouds. It was a holiday on the first Monday after Good Friday. It was even funnier to watch kites flutter and fall to the ground because someone had cut their tails by another kite flyer who put a razor blade at the end of his/her kite tail. Sometimes the kites got entangled with others while flying too close together. These would also fall and get damaged. Damaged kites cannot fly again unless we repaired them. At the end of the day, the kites were taken down, if possible. Some kites were stored for the following year and some joined the rubbish heap while others decorated the power lines and tall trees. We did not always get a kite to fly on Easter Monday. Sometimes we made kites by removing some pointers from the broom and pasting them on kite paper. There were several designs and sizes of kites, from the simple to the exotic. The fabulous kites were only a representation of a large array of Guyanese creative masterpieces. Sometimes the kites were so exotic, they could not get them off the ground to fly.

Kwekwe

Let's turn our attention to another cultural tradition. Kwekwe is a wedding eve tradition in Guyana. I experienced this in unique forms in other parts of the country. I believe this was an African tradition of bringing together the families and friends of the bride and groom in a joyous celebration. The process might have been different, but the folk songs and the lewd dancing and vulgar singing and behavior were the same. In some parts of the country, the bride's family traveled to meet the groom's family. In other parts, it was reversed. Yet in some parts, they just had a Kwekwe, with both families together. Sometimes the bride and groom would play games such as "hide and seek." There was always food and drinking during the night.

This activity took place during the night until the wee hours of the morning. It was fun for those who enjoyed a good kwekwe. I only experienced a kwekwe when I was grown. Mama never allowed me to go to the kwekwe. I could only attend the wedding and reception. She said that kwekwe was not for children. Anyway, as long as I was in the house or in the vicinity of a kwekwe, being as curious as I was, you know exactly what I was doing? Yes! Peeping, as I always did. That's how I knew what happened at a kwekwe during my childhood. Incidentally, every home I visited, whether large or small, had creases in the walls and there were other children doing the same thing—peeping.

Music, Song and Dance

Folk Songs of Guyana: This is a small sample of our Folk Songs. They are sung at Kwekwes, at nights while camping or during a concert. These songs are very rhythmic and the dancing and gyrations are "out of this world." I would love to be a fly on the wall to hear you read or try to sing these songs. They are good tongue twisters.

Kuma-Kuma Fish

Nah eat ah fish, mama
Nah eat ah fish
Ah Kuma-Kuma fish, mama,
Nah eat ah fish

He worse than perai, mama
Worse than perai
Ah Kuma-Kuma fish, mama
Nah eat ah fish

He guh bring you bad luck, mama
Bring you bad luck
Ah Kuma-Kuma fish, mama
Nah eat ah fish!

He guh wok you belly, mama
Wok you belly
Ah Kuma-Kuma fish, mama
Nah eat ah fish

This song cautions the guests about the consequences of eating spoiled or poisonous fish.

****

UNCLE JOE

Me bin a' rice fiel' go wok, me na hear when manin' train pass
Me bin a' rice fiel' go wok, me na hear when manin' train pass
Uncle Joe, gimme mo leh me go, Uncle Joe, gimme mo leh me go
Uncle Joe, gimme mo leh me go, Uncle Joe, gimme mo leh me go

Me bin a' cane fiel' go cut, me na hear when manin' train pass
Me bin a' cane fiel' go cut, me na hear when manin' train pass
Uncle Joe, gimme mo leh me go, Uncle Joe, gimme mo leh me go
Uncle Joe, gimme mo leh me go, Uncle Joe, gimme mo leh me go

Me bin a' punt trench go swim, an de watah cool dung me skin
Me bin a' punt trench go swim, an de watah cool dung me skin
Uncle Joe, gimme mo leh me go, Uncle Joe, gimme mo leh me go
Uncle Joe, gimme mo leh me go, Uncle Joe, gimme mo leh me go

This song presents different scenarios – The rice and cane harvesters who missed the train early in the morning are requesting another train service to take them to work in the fields. Uncle Joe happened to be the boss man. Then, the last stanza speaks of swimming in the punt trench after work because of the cooling effect of the water. They missed the last train and are requesting another train service to take them home. The punt trench was found in the cane and rice fields.

****

MANIN' NEIGHBA

Manin' neighba, manin', Manin' neighba, manin' Manin' neighba, manin', ah don' want yuh conniving ma-nin' Manin' neighba, manin', Manin' neighba, manin'
Manin' neighba, manin', yuh can keep yuh conniving manin'

When yuh been ah Kurupung, Yuh na bin tell me manin'
Now because yuh money done, yuh come wid yuh conniving mannin
When yuh had yuh pocket full, Yuh na bin tell me manin'
Now because yuh money done, yuh hustle fuh tell me manin'

Chorus:

Neighba neighba Joe come, Neighba neighba Joe come
Neighba neighba Joe come, Dis all de money dat e' wok fo'
Two poun' note an a guilda piece, Two poun' note an a guilda piece,
Two poun' note an a guilda piece, Dis all de money dat e' wok fo'

Chorus:

Ow Joseph, poor me, Ow Joseph, poor me,
Ow Joseph, poor me, wha' me go do wid a guilda piece?
One bunch green plantain, one string kakwari
One gill black pepper, all da can buy wid a
guilda piece (back to the beginning)

This song tells of a gold miner who came home after working in Kurupung. This is found in the interior of Guyana. It is rich in mineral resources. After mining the gold and diamond, the miners usually make a lot of money. Neighbors look forward to get some of this money when the men come home. However, this time the miner did not give out any money to his neighbors. They become enraged and "tell him off." This poor man tried to tell them that he did not make much money. All he had was two pounds (British currency) and a guilder (Suriname currency). This money could not buy much groceries for himself. But the neighbors did not listen to him.

Other songs in Guyana include Soca, Calypso and Reggae. The steel band is also a favorite musical instrument in Guyana and the Caribbean. These songs are also sung throughout the Caribbean.

****

Guyana's Independence and Becoming a Republic

I was in elementary school when Guyana became an independent nation on May 26, 1966. We were taught the significance of this achievement. This meant we were no longer under the umbrella of the United Kingdom or Great Britain. We were shown our new flag, which was called the Golden Arrow Head and were taught the significance of each color. We also got our own Coat of Arms and National Anthem. We were also free to make our own laws to govern our country. The name was then changed from British Guiana to Guyana. The official language remained the same - English. However, there are other languages spoken by some of our natives.

Four years later, on February 23, 1970 Guyana became a Republic. This meant that Guyana exonerated its relationship with the British Monarchy, while keeping its membership with the Commonwealth of Nations. The Prime Minister, Honorable Linden Forbes Sampson Burnham became the first President and declared Guyana to be a Socialist Country. The name was changed again to the Cooperative Republic of Guyana.

As Guyana was going through its metamorphosis, everything seemed to be changing at an enormous rate. Life as we know it changed drastically.

The President wanted us to become self-sufficient so important foods were banned. We no longer had access to wheat flour, imported oil, milk and other necessities. Instead, we were left to create foods from our locally grown products such as rice flour and use coconut oil. Long food lines became the norm as food supplies became scarce. Since I did most of the shopping for our home, it was my job to stand on line for food. Adapting to the new social norm was not easy, but Guyanese are strong and resilient. We found ways to get what we wanted. This new social order ushered in new forms of entrepreneurships as Guyanese scoured neighboring countries including the United States to purchase scarce food items to be sold for enormous profits. The demand became more than the supply. This trade was illegal since the items had to be smuggled into the country for local consumption. Further, when the traders were caught, the items were confiscated and burned. This of course gave rise to bribery and corruption. Meanwhile, the different entities in the country began to prosper and develop in different ways - agriculture, housing, the military, education, and the mining industries began to boom. It was predicted that Guyana would be the food basket of the Caribbean.

A Wake

I remember my aunt saying "That was a good wake" whenever she returned home from a wake. I think she was talking about the food and drink she consumed during the evening. She never took anything seriously, anyway. Whenever a person died, there was usually a wake. During this event, many of the deceased friends and family gather in the home to offer support, comfort and sympathy. There was also singing of hymns, eating and drinking. The burial can be within a few days to a few weeks depending on the circumstances. If the deceased has relatives abroad, then the burial will take longer, awaiting the arrival of the relatives. A wake was held every night all night long before the funeral and burial took place.

The funeral service was either held in a church or the cemetery, although it was not uncommon for the funeral service to be held at the home of the deceased. After the service, the funeral procession moved slowly down Main Street with the hearse in the lead, followed by cars and people on foot. The procession usually passed by the deceased's home on the way to the cemetery.

After the deceased has passed away, there is the nine-night event. This is a more joyous occasion. It was held on the ninth night after the deceased has passed away. The next event in this series is the forty-night. Not everyone observed this event. I do not know the significance of these events.

Mashramani Celebrations

When Guyana obtained its independence from Great Britain and later became a Republic, it gave birth to Mashramani also called Mash. It's an Amerindian word meaning "A celebration after the harvest." This celebration consisted of steel band and calypso music, marching or tramping in the streets, floats, food, drinking and revelry. Mashramani is also considered a Caribbean Carnival because of its similarities. We hold it on February 23rd each year. Many Guyanese from all over the world go home for this celebration. It's an enjoyable time to meet friends and family that you haven't seen in several years. I only took an active part in Mashramani once as a child. It was so much fun as we proudly displayed our new flag and danced to calypso music on our float.

The floats in the Mashramani celebrations were themed and depicted some aspect of the proud Guyanese culture, whether it was displaying the many racial heritages or proudly displaying the beautiful sceneries and natural resources in Guyana. It was a time when Guyanese from all racial and cultural heritage came together for a time of joyful integration.

Box Hand

This is another means of saving money. A group of people of any amount, maybe six, eight, ten and so on come together to put their money in a pool. The amount of money and the duration of time was agreed upon by the participants. I have never seen Mama participating in this activity. I learned about the box from my friends and later when I was employed, I participated. This is how it works:

- One box holder was appointed (someone whom the group trusted) to hold and distribute the funds.

- Each member had the privilege to choose which hand or the time they wanted to draw their money or draw numbers to make this an organized process.

- Members gave their money to the box holder who then distributed the money.

- For example, let us suppose ten people come together to put one hundred dollars per month each. Therefore, the box hand lasted for ten months and each person would draw one thousand dollars when it was their turn. Some people gave the box holder a tip when they received their money.

- The box can be held daily, weekly or monthly depending on the group.

- It would not work if anyone dropped out of the box when they received their money. So, only people who could be trusted were allowed to join the box.

- Later, when I immigrated to North America, I learned that the box was also called SuSu.

Burial Society

Death is inevitable in every society and burial costs could be astronomical. The way this worked was a large number of people came together either weekly or monthly and subscribed a small amount of money to the pool. Each member's contribution was decided by the committee members. When a member died, the funeral expenses were paid by the burial society. At the end of the year, the excess funds were distributed equitably among the members.

Mama was a member of the burial society. Every week she paid her dues and at the end of the year, she collected her bonus. This money came at the right time because it helped us to prepare for Christmas.

Foods from Guyana–A Culinary Delight

Every country and culture have its foods. With Guyana, many of our foods are unique to our country. Some of our foods are also unique to the Caribbean. However, most of our foods have their origins in Africa, India, China, Europe, and through the ingenuity of African slaves and East Indian indentured laborers. The Amerindians, who were the original people of Guyana, have contributed much to our cuisine; making us a true "Melting Pot."

- Many of our main dishes, baked goods and snacks are served on special occasions such as weddings, holidays, parties and religious ceremonies.

- Even though these foods are unique to most of the country, as you go from region to region, the names may be different, and there are other original foods that are unique to that region.

Below I have listed a small sample of popular foods that are part of our culture. The list is not exhaustive, since Guyanese are very good at creating foods from whatever ingredients are available to us. As a child, Mama made all of these foods. Many of them took several hours to make. This was not a problem, since I was always there to help her. For example, her split peas soups on Sundays took about four hours to cook. Her cook-up rice took about two to three hours depending on the ingredients she used. Her pepper pot took several days. She boiled it every day until it met with her approval. We cooked on a coal pot or fireside.

Brief Food Facts from Guyana

Curries: Made with Indian spices including garam masala, Gera, turmeric, onion, garlic and more. Guyanese prepare various types of curries. They include curries in many of our main dishes. We put curries in vegetables, meats, and seafood and some side dishes or snacks such as channa (chick peas).

Cook-Up-Rice: A delicious rice dish, cooked with coconut milk, peas, and a variety of meats and fish or shrimp - fresh or dried. We use a variety of seasonings for flavor. There are many variations to this dish. Instead of peas, spinach, okra, or cabbage can be used. It just depends on the availability of ingredients and the choice of the cook. It is often said that cook-up-rice is made with everything but the kitchen sink.

Chow Mein: Made with chow mien noodles, vegetables, meat, shrimp, along with Chinese spices.

Roti: A flat bread made with flour, baking powder, oil or ghee and water. It is baked on a tawa. It can also be made in a large frying pan.

Dahl Pouri/Puri: Another flat bread. The roti dough is filled with a mixture of ground split peas and Indian spices. It is baked on a Tawa.

Channa (Chick Peas): Is boiled until tender, strained and then stewed with Indian spices. It can also be soaked, drained, pat dried and fried until it becomes crispy.

Dumplings and Bakes: Basically, made from the same material which is flour, margarine, baking powder, salt, sugar water or milk. Dumplings are either steamed or placed in soups. Bakes are fried or baked in the oven, on a tawa or in a covered pan on the stove.

Floats: Made with bread dough. Black pepper can be added (optional). The dough is made into tiny balls, flattened and allowed to rise again. They are fried in deep oil. While frying, the dough rises to the top forming a large air pocket. They are served with fish, eggs or eaten as is. They are essentially bakes.

Salt Fish: made from different types of fish which is salted and dried. Before cooking, it is soaked for several hours or boiled to remove most of the salt. The fish can be roasted, stewed, placed in a batter to make fritters, mixed with potatoes to make cakes, placed in cook-up-rice or (metage, metem or metemge). Sometimes it is cooked with vegetables. The versatility of salt fish is endless.

Fufu: Made from green plantains. The plantain is boiled and when it is cooled, it is pounded with a mortar and pestle until very fine, and then formed into balls. The fufu is usually eaten with soups. These days, I make fufu in a food processor instead of a mortar and pestle.

Fish: There is a wide variety of fish in Guyana. Fish is a staple of our diet. It is cooked in various ways and used in several dishes. It is stewed, curried, baked, fried, steamed and made into cakes. It is used with vegetables and greens such as calalu or spinach and many more.

Soups: There are so many soup dishes. Soups are made with different types of peas such as split peas, black eye peas, pigeon peas and more. We also use various types of vegetables in our soups. Usually, soups contain meat, fish head or vegetables. Sometimes it may contain cow heel (feet), pig trotters (feet), tripe or any other part of the animal that the cook desires to use. It is normal to include vegetables such as plantains, cassava, sweet potatoes, yams and more. Soups are eaten as a meal instead of a side dish.

Pepperpot: A variety of meats are cooked with cassareep (a sauce made from cassava juice and sugar). A variety of spices are also used. It is not unusual for pepper pot to be cooked for several days. The longer it cooks, the better it gets. This is a "must-have" dish at Christmas.

Garlic Pork: Pork is cleaned and soaked in vinegar, salt, garlic and hot peppers for several days. It is then removed, washed, pat dried, thinly sliced and fried. This is a "must-have" dish at Christmas.

Porridges: Porridges were usually eaten for breakfast and sometimes for dinner. There are several types of porridges such as oatmeal, cassava, rice, cornmeal, plantain, flour, sago, and barley. Porridges are usually made with water, regular milk or coconut milk, spices and sugar. Spices in Guyana does not include peppers. Popular spices are cinnamon, nutmeg and cloves.

Cou cou: A dish made with cornmeal, coconut milk, okra and seasonings. Sometimes salt beef is included.

Cassava Bread: This is flat bread made with cassava. The cassava is grated, washed and squeezed to remove the starches and excess water. This excess water is then left to sit for several hours (over-night). The water is drained into a large pot, while the sediment which is a creamy white substance is dried in the sun. This is dried in clumps and can be pounded into a powdery substance. This is boiled and becomes starch and can be used on clothing. The cassava juice/water, however, is boiled until it becomes a dark brown substance called cassareep. This cassareep is used in stews, and to make pepper pot. The husk of the cassava is pounded in a mortar and pestle until it becomes fine. It is sifted and then removed a little at a time and spread on a tawa to bake on both sides. This is then placed in the sun to dry. After this process, it becomes dry and crispy. Cassava bread is used with pepper pot or dunked in teas.

Quinches: These are made like Cassava Bread. A small round cutter (about four to five inches in diameter) is used. The cutter is placed on the tawa, and the cassava husk is placed in it to form a circle. A sweet, grated coconut filling made with spices and sugar is cooked and placed on each circle. The circle is then folded over and sealed to make a semi-circle. They are baked on both sides.

Bread: Similar to many types of bread around the world. Made with flour, water, yeast, sugar, salt, butter (margarine), shortening (lard) and sometimes coconut milk. It is sometimes braided then baked in an oven.

Butter Flaps: These are made with the same bread dough. They are rolled into balls and flattened with a rolling pin. Butter or margarine is spread over the surface, and the dough is folded into a triangle. They are baked in an oven.

Tennis Rolls: Sweet bread dough, with special essences. The dough is made into balls and baked in an oven.

Sweet Bread: There are several types of sweet bread. They are either made with yeast or baking powder. They can be made with one fruit or a combination of mixed fruits, currants, raisins, grated coconut or cherries, sometimes milk and eggs are used.

Patties: Made with short crust pastry dough and ground meat (beef, chicken or turkey) filling. The filling is seasoned and cooked. The dough is rolled out and cut in circles. The filling is placed in the center of the dough. Special patty baking pans are used.

Cheese Rolls: These are also made with short crust pastry dough. The dough is rolled out and cut into oblong pieces. Cheese is seasoned and place in the center of each piece of dough. The filled dough is rolled, placed on a baking sheet and baked in an oven.

Pine Tarts: These are also made with short crust pastry dough. The filling is made of grated pineapple, sugar and spices. The dough is rolled out and cut in circles. The pineapple filling is placed in the center. The dough is shaped into triangles and baked in an oven.

Note: An egg wash is placed over the Patties, Cheese Rolls and Pine Tarts before they are baked.

Buns: There are different types of buns: Example—Coconut Buns: made with grated coconut, sugar, baking powder, raisins (optional), margarine, water or milk, flour and eggs. Rock Buns: made without raisins or coconut. **Cherry Buns:** made without raisins or coconut and with a cherry in the middle.

Cassava Pone: Made with Cassava, coconut, spices, sugar, black pepper (optional), water or milk. The batter is poured into a square or oblong pan and baked. After baking, the cassava pone is cut into squares before serving.

Corn Pone: Made with cornmeal, grated coconut, sugar, flour, eggs, milk and baking powder. The batter is poured into a square or oblong pan and baked. After baking, the pone is cut into squares before serving.

Fat Top: Made with cornmeal, coconut milk, sugar and spices. This mixture is poured in a baking pan and baked in the oven. While baking, the fat from the coconut milk rises to the top. This is better when served warm.

Roly Poly (also called Salara): Made with the bread dough. Coconut is grated and cooked with red food coloring, sugar and spices. The dough is rolled out, and the filling is spread on the surface. The dough and filling are rolled up and sealed. It is placed on a baking sheet and baked. After baking, it is cut into two to three-inch slices before serving. Sometimes the filling is not colored.

Sponge Cake: This is not a true "sponge cake." I guess it gets its name because of its "spongy" texture. It is made with flour, sugar, eggs, (milk – optional), essence, baking powder, margarine or butter. The batter is poured in a baking pan and baked.

Conkie: Made with cornmeal, crushed ripe bananas, pumpkin or plantains, sugar, grated coconut, spices and (raisins - optional). This mixture is placed on green banana or plantain leaves which are folded and tied. The conkie is placed in boiling water to boil until firm. This is better when served warm.

Shine Rice: Rice cooked with coconut milk and sometimes with salt beef/pork.

Polouri/Pholourie: Made with flour, curry, pepper, (split peas - optional), baking powder or yeast, water, salt and seasonings. They are formed into small balls and fried in deep fat. They are served with savory mango or tamarind sauce.

Sugar Cakes: There are many types of sugar Cakes. They are made with coconut, sugar and spices. They can be colored red or white. They can be grated or chipped. They can also be brown, made with brown sugar.

Mithai: Made with flour, yeast or baking powder, salt, spices, water or milk, margarine and sugar. The dough is made and allowed to rise. It is then rolled out and cut into three to four-inch strips and fried. A syrup is made and poured on the mithai.

Cheese Straws: Made with flour, cheese, salt, pepper and baking powder (optional). They can be fluted through a cookie cutter or rolled out and cut into strips.

Amchar/Achar: Usually made with grated green mangoes. Although bilimbi/sourie/lady finger is also used. This mixture is mixed with salt, pepper, garam masala and mustard oil.

Guava Jelly/Jam: Made with Guava, sugar and spices.

Tamarind Sauce – Savory and Sweet. For the savory sauce, the tamarind is boiled with salt, pepper and water until it thickens. For the sweet sauce, the tamarind is boiled with sugar, sometimes pepper, and water until it thickens.

Tamarind Balls – Made with tamarind, lots of sugar, pepper, and salt.

Plantain Chips: This is made mainly with green plantains. Yellow plantains are seldom used. The plantains are sliced thinly and fried in deep oil until crispy. They are lightly salted when finished

Guyanese Beverages

Fruit Drinks and Wines: Guyanese are known for making delicious homemade drinks and wines. These thirst quenchers are made from any local fruit and water. Fruits include tamarind, passion fruit, five fingers (star fruit), limes, lemons, bilimbi, pineapple and many more. The drinks are made fresh or "set," left to ferment for two to three days. After the pineapple skin is cut, the meat is eaten and the drink is made from the skins. Sugar and spices such as cinnamon sticks and cloves are added to give the drinks their characteristic flavors and aromas. The drinks are strained and served with ice. As a child, lemonade or swank and lime drink were the easiest drink to make and usually the go-to drink when you are thirsty and wanted to drink something other than water. We couldn't always afford to buy sweet drink or soda. Limes, lemons and sugar were cheap.

Wines are made in a similar manner as the homemade drinks, except the mixture is left to ferment for about three to four weeks. Homemade wines are made from fruits such as gooseberry and jamun. Rice is also used to make wine. Water is also added along with sugar and spices for flavor. I was not allowed to drink wine as a child and no explanation was given. All I was told was, "Don't drink that," or "Wine is not for children." You know what I was doing when no one was at home! Yes, tasting the wine! I was curious and just couldn't help myself.

Bush Rum: This was popular and also illegal when I was growing up in Guyana. Whenever Uncle Andy came home to Mama's house, he talked about bush rum and had his friends bring some for him. He seldom drank with friends. Most times he drank alone and made sure it was finished before he left.

The ingredients and process for making this liquor are closely guarded secrets. No one spoke openly about it; I believe for fear of being arrested for its possession and consumption. I think my uncle and others were intrigued by the fact that they could obtain and consume it without being caught. I often heard Uncle Andy said, "this is better than D'Aguiar." Now, D'Aguiar was a legal manufacturer of alcoholic products. He owned a legal distillery. As I got older, I learned that bush rum has a very high alcohol content and can be lethal. I am glad the odor turned me off and I couldn't try it as a child.

Eggnog: Also called cogue. This is a drink made with milk, eggs, sugar and spices. It is sometimes laced with alcohol. Mama gave us warm eggnog sometimes on Sunday morning. This was a treat and it was delicious. She added rum to her eggnog before she drank it.

The Day I Met My Father

Dear Father,

There is a little girl who feels a sense of loss, never knowing who her father is or who he might have been. She has never known a father's voice, a father's touch, or a father's love. This little girl knew that her father existed, but was never privileged to grace his ominous presence, but once. She never got to call him dad.

Have you ever thought about the little girl whom you have brought into this world? Where she is? Or what might have happened to her? Did she grow into a woman that you would be proud to say "this is my daughter?" Is your heart longing to see her? Would you like to introduce her to your children and friends? Are you going to leave this world never knowing who your little girl is? Or what she has grown up to be? Do you think about her?

From your long-lost daughter.

Ingrid

Triumphs of a Little Girl

I now turn my attention to my absent father. My grandmother allowed us to play under the tiny porch (landing) only when she was at home. One day as I was playing under the porch alone, I saw a tall dark-skinned man climbing the stairs; we looked at each other but said nothing. This was a stranger I have never met. A few minutes later my grandmother called me into the house and said, "This is your father." I was about ten years old and was seeing him for the first time. I sat on the floor and gazed up at him. He did not hug me or even give me a kiss or hold me. He never expressed any form of emotion towards me. I did not know if he was happy to see me. He said "Your grandmother will take good care of you. Write and let me know what you want." I said, "Yes, sir." Mama said, "You can go back and play," so I left. A few minutes later, I saw him walking down the stairs. While he was leaving, he never turned around to say, "goodbye." He never asked me how I was doing in school or anything. He never gave me an encouraging word or a hug. This was the first and only time I saw my father. Imagine again! I am carrying the last name of a man I do not know. Several months later, my mother told me that he used to visit me when I was a baby and left his son, who was about five years older than me, on the street to wait for him.

Since my father dearest wanted me to let him know what I wanted, I wrote him a letter at his request. The package came a few weeks later. He sent me a pair of white socks, a pair of white patent leather shoes that were a little big, a singlet, two pairs of panties and a cream to rub on my skin to remove the mosquito bite marks. My grandmother stuffed the front of the shoe with paper. This was my first and only gifts from him.

This brings me to my godmother. She had about five children. She lived not too far away from me. Every Sunday afternoon, I rode to her house on a bicycle that Mama got from her employer when she worked in Watooka. After I got there, my god sisters and I rode to Sunday school at the Anglican Church. After Sunday school, we went to their godparents who were wealthy and well known in our town. They gave us snacks and gifts, occasionally.

After attending Sunday school for some time, they selected us for confirmation as was the religious custom of the church. This was a direct path for membership. My godmother also called Nen Nen bought my dress, bible and veil; I was proud to wear my shoes, socks, and underwear which my father sent me. I got my picture taken at this special event; I felt on top of the world. Every Saturday, I cleaned my only pair of church shoes with Blanco—white shoe polish in anticipation of my Sunday afternoon routine. One Sunday afternoon after showing up at Nen Nen's house, she told me that my father was there. Imagine that confused look on my face because I did not know what to do with this information. I stood there and said nothing. This happened several times. I wondered why he did not come to see me. The more I thought about this calamity, the more perplexed I became. It was mind-boggling to a ten-year-old. Why would he go out of his way to see my godmother and not come to see me? I was his child. I later learned that they transferred him to the Berbice River area. He had to travel through New Amsterdam where I lived to get there. Then I got to thinking—now he lived in Georgetown and worked in the Berbice River. He had to travel to Rosignol, then take the Torani Ferry to cross the Berbice River. When he came off the ferry in New Amsterdam, he had to pass where I lived to get to the next ferry (the Čanjie Pheasant) in Stanleytown to go up to the other part of the Berbice River. He went out of his way to visit my godmother regularly, and when he left her home, he had to pass where I lived again. There was no other way to do it.

Please check my diagram (in the work book) to see if you can help my father find his little girl. I lived in a small town with three major roads and several parallel and connecting streets. I concluded he did not want to see me; he did not care about me and did not want me in his life. Perhaps he felt that if he came to see me, then he would have to contribute to my well-being, and he wanted none of that. Maybe that's the reason Mama never mentioned him at all. I thought, "Why didn't Nen Nen ask him to come and see me?" She lived with her husband, and her children were able to be with their father every day.

The inevitable happened one Sunday afternoon during my regular visit. My god sisters said to me as soon as I arrived, "Ingrid is going to punish." Once again, I was dumb stricken and said nothing. As soon as I went home, I told Mama what happened, and she said, "Don't bother with them." I told her I did not want to go back there. I felt this was an insult, and they did not wish me well and thought I would suffer, for reasons unknown to me. This was very uncomfortable for me. This ended my relationship with my godmother and her children. I did not know what someone said in their presence, but from a child's point of view, this was not good and I recognized it. My grandmother never forced me to do anything when I did not want to do it. She was always on my side.

Meanwhile, I continued to attend church on Sunday morning mass at ten o'clock when most young people attended. I made a few friends here. We went on trips and camps during the holidays. My grandmother, however, chose my friends. She did not allow me to go out with friends if she did not know their parents. Imagine my calamity when a friend invited me to a birthday party and I could not go. I did not have any parties.

Mama usually made a cake, pastries, and sometimes ice cream for my birthday. We celebrated this occasion among ourselves at home. The next day, she gave me a bag of goodies to take to my teachers.

My Confirmation – Age Ten-Eleven
I am wearing the dress and veil (Nen Nen) made for me.
She also gave me the bible.
My father sent me the socks, shoes and underwear.
I washed and styled my hair.
Mama gave me the jewelry.

Getting back to my father's package: I wore out my white patent leather shoes he sent me. I had to remove the paper stuffed in front of my shoes because I was outgrowing them. A little hole appeared at the bottom while the rest of the sole became thin. The heels were almost invisible. I became very creative. I promptly cut two pieces of cardboard to the shape of the sole and placed them inside the shoes. This only solved part of my problem. While I could get to church, I could not take communion. To do this meant that I had to go to the altar and kneel. This was too embarrassing. Everyone would see my "sole-less" shoes and make fun of me. I could not let that happen. I had to choose between church and friends. I chose the church because I believed that it was more important. I did not want to tell Mama about my shoes because I knew she could not afford to purchase a new pair. I told her I would go to the early mass at six o'clock in the morning, instead of ten o'clock. Few people attended the six o'clock mass. They were much older and most of them were coming from work or had to go to work. It was dark and no one could see the bottom of my shoes. This continued for several months until I could no longer wear my shoes. Imagine my calamity when it rained on Sunday mornings! My grandmother later bought me another pair of shoes. I wondered if my father ever thought about me. Did he think that the gifts he sent me would last forever and not need replenishing?

My father became a mystery and nothing but the tiniest speck, probably an atom on my memory. To this day, I have never seen him again. If I did, I could not recognize him. I later heard that he was working at Eve Larry Police Station. When I attended College in Georgetown, I had to pass where he worked. I did the same thing he did – "pass on by." I never stopped by to say hello. I didn't know him. Further, I did not want him to think I wanted something from him, or I wanted to disrupt his "perfect" family life.

Several years later, after I was grown, it must have been at least fifteen years later, my mother told Mama that she met my father and he told her he heard that I was a whore on the streets. My mother knew that I was working very hard, and that I went to college and was a science teacher, but she chose not to say anything to him. I had no reason or intention to prostitute myself. I went to college tuition free. I got a grant from the government in exchange for a four-year contract to serve my country when I left college. Further, Uncle Andy always brought food and money for me while I was in college. I also did hairdressing regularly for my friends to earn a little more money. I had more money than I needed.

Moving forward, several years after I left Guyana for the Caribbean and subsequently for the USA, I heard that my mother met my father again, and he told her the same nonsense again, and as usual, she said nothing in my defense. Meanwhile, I was working on getting my BS degree. I came to the USA every summer to attend college for two years. The certificate I got from Teacher's College in Guyana was only equivalent to an Associate Degree here in the USA.

When I immigrated to the USA, I worked even harder. I worked full time during the day as a science teacher, and I went to college at nights. The days when I was not in college, I had a part-time job in a daycare center. On a few weekends, I would fill in for a friend as a Home Health Aid. When school was closed during the summer months, I had a summer job during the day and went to college at nights. I even became a real estate sales agent to make a little more money. For several years I did not go on vacations. All I did was work and go to college.

I do not think a prostitute would invest so much time on work and education. I wondered what motivated him to be so eager to berate me, but was not motivated to support me as a child! Once again, I must wonder about the condition of the human heart. Since my father heard such horrifying news about me, one would think he would try to rescue me or at least try to find and help me. He did nothing but repeated the negative information to my mother. She once again listened and accepted this information. I wondered who these people were? Was my father making things up to make him look good? Was he trying to justify his inaction and errant behavior towards me? What's the point, anyway? He couldn't pick me out in a crowd even if we came face to face. The answer is simple… "You are berating someone you don't even know." Someone who has worked very hard to make her life a success. Why didn't my mother defend me when she knew the truth? What "great parents" I have! Many parents would be proud to have a child like me but not mine. This is mind-boggling, and I am dumbfounded again. I cannot adequately describe how I feel, so I will leave it alone.

In the workbook, there is a diagram of my father's path to and from work. I lived in a small town. There were three major streets. Water Street—which was the easiest path to and from work—Main Street in the middle and Town Savannah/Savannah Park or Back Dam at the end. Several intersection streets were running through these three streets. Mr. R. Benjamin went out of his way to visit my godmother and her family. Any of the three major streets could have taken him to my grandmother's house. He had to pass our house and street. There was no other way for him to get to and from work, they laid the town out like a rectangle.

Life Lessons I Learned From My Grandmother

Mama was a beacon of light to my young life. She made me think about life in ways that I could not understand until I stopped and thought about the messages she was trying to convey.

Unique and sometimes crude in her ways, she spoke with authority and purpose. I had no other choice but to pay attention whenever she spoke.

Mama was not a very talkative person. Most times, she would not verbalize her feelings. Instead, she would roll her eyes and give me "that disapproving look" whenever she perceived that something was amiss. Even though she was of few words, whenever she spoke, it was very poignant, substantive, engaging and full of wisdom. She often expressed that she disliked "idle gossip." Sometimes I think she was ahead of her time by the things she said and did.

I remembered that as a child, there were no role models for me in my immediate environment. Sure, there were my teachers and other influential people in my hometown whom I admired. But there was an intense fire burning inside me, something more like an intense desire to develop into something greater than my present circumstances. I had to create a different path and one that was all my own.

For several years, I thought my grandmother was my role-model. Then I realized that she was not the total package I would like to be my role model. A role model is someone whom you admire, someone whom you look up to, and someone whom you desire to emulate in every way. I loved, admired and looked up to Mama, but I did not want to emulate her in every way. She was a domestic servant. There is nothing wrong with this career choice. If I had to do this line of work for my survival, I would do it. During my grandmother's time, there were few choices for a woman, if she were married. Mama wanted to be a teacher, but, after her mother's death, she left home, met my grandfather, got married and became a housewife. However, this was not my passion. I wanted more. I wanted something different for myself while Mama made all the sacrifices that made it possible for me to achieve the success, I sought for myself. My grandmother was my first teacher, cheerleader and life coach. She not only taught me how to cook and clean and the necessity for good grooming and deportment; she taught me lessons that were far superior to what I could have learned in any educational institution. This was priceless!

She was a very principled person. For example, one afternoon her friend Mr. Edwards came to visit. I believe he was her boyfriend because whenever he came over, she sent Carol and me into the bedroom, then she turned up the radio, so we couldn't hear anything. It rained that day when he came over, so our yard was wet and muddy. By the time he was ready to leave that night, it was dark and almost impossible to navigate through the mud on the planks laid out to walk on without getting our shoes muddy. All the planks did not have the same width, length, and thickness. If one was not familiar with the layout of the yard, you could get hurt. So, my grandmother, being kind, lent Mr. Edwards her torch (flash) light. She said to him, "I am lending you this torchlight, bring it back tomorrow." He took the torchlight and waded his way out of the yard without incident.

Well, tomorrow came and went. The following days and weeks went by. There was no torchlight and no Mr. Edwards. Every time she saw him in the streets, she accosted him for her torchlight. He promised to return it, and as usual, he ignored her. Then one day, Mama went to court and got a writ of summons for her torchlight. This was unbelievable but true. I couldn't make this up even if I tried. On the court day she told the magistrate she lent Mr. Edwards her torchlight, he did not return it, and that she would like to have her torchlight back. The magistrate just couldn't believe what he was hearing, so he asked her to repeat it. She said the same thing again. He asked Mr. Edwards if this was true. Mr. Edwards said, "Yes your honor." The magistrate wanted to give her the value of the torchlight. My grandmother said, "Your honor, all I want is my torchlight back." The magistrate looked at her, shook his head slowly from left to right and ordered Mr. Edwards to return the torchlight. It so happened that Mr. Edwards had the torchlight in his possession in court. He immediately turned it over to my grandmother and said, 'Thank you." The judge settled the case in Mama's favor. We all walked out of the court. She never waited for the magistrate to close the case. I remembered hearing the magistrate saying, "Case closed." When I looked back, he hit his desk with what appeared to be a small mallet. I later learned that they called it a gavel. Mr. Edwards and my grandmother never spoke again.

Later that evening, when Tita, my aunt, came home, she asked Mama why she took Mr. Edwards to court for a torchlight. She asked her why didn't she just buy another torchlight, because it was inexpensive. Mama said, "It's not the torchlight, it is the principle behind it. I told him to bring back my torchlight, but he kept it," as she waved her index finger in the air and nodded her head from side to side. She seemed very angry even though her torchlight was returned.

When I think about this story, I wonder if it was worth the trouble, because both Mama and Mr. Edwards lost a day of work and not to mention their pay, and they wasted the court's time over something as insignificant as a cheap torchlight. I lost half a day of school because I was her witness, even though I did not see when she gave him the torchlight. Mama told me what happened when she became angry because he did not return her torchlight. My grandmother, however, seemed to be vindicated and justified. I guess it worked for her. She won her case and got her torchlight back. Further, Mr. Edwards could have returned the torchlight, he passed our house every day.

What I learned from this episode is that not everything is worth fighting for, pick your battles, and fight for what you believe in. The next thing was, "the black man borrows but once." This is what Mama often said. This is because some people never returned what they borrowed in the first place, so they cannot return a second time. The last thing is that "lend nothing you cannot afford to lose," because the borrower may never return the item. It may be necessary to resort to extreme measures to be repaid for what someone owes you.

In this world, Mama always said there are people who "hang their hats where their hands can't reach to take it down." As a child, I did not understand what she was saying. As an adult, when I think about it, she meant—do not live above your means. Living above one's means can lead to serious financial problems that may be hard to overcome.

Mama was always saying that the neighbors needed to "get some ambition." Our neighbors gambled all day long. I guess this meant that they needed to seek a career, develop themselves and earn an honest day's pay. She encouraged me to study and get an education so I would be independent and not depend on anyone for sustenance.

When my neighbor Charlotte tormented me daily, I told my grandmother. She never approached Charlotte or complained to her parents. She took me to a top attorney who was her nephew, to get a letter to have Charlotte to desist from taunting me. After receiving the letter, Charlotte never bothered me again.

This incident taught me not to allow anyone to define who I am, what I should become or how I should live my life. I should have the strength to stand up to a bully. I do not have to get into a fistfight with anyone and get down to their level; I can take the higher road. There are several means of resolving problems. Also, it may be very difficult to reason with some people. So, you may have to resolve the issue the best way you can.

Mama taught me to set goals and work hard to achieve them in her way. She made me realize that my present circumstances should not be the only determinant for my future. Living in the ghetto should not be my destiny. She exposed me to different lifestyles and kept me well guarded by monitoring my friendships and my extracurricular activities. She was over-protective of me. Her favorite phrase "show me your company and I'll tell you who you are" still rings in my ears. Friendships and associations influence us and may cause us to act out of our character. Our friends or who we associate with are a representation of us. If a person wants to judge your character, they need only to look at who your friends are. I did not listen to or understand what this meant until it was too late. After being betrayed by friends and being hurt, I realized that the signs were right there all along. I either did not want to see it, or I did not want to experience the loss of someone whom I thought was a friend. Guess what? It all came back, and it hurt more when I realized that I had kept and sustained those friendships for a long time, just to find out those friends were betrayers. What makes the wound even deeper is that I let those persons into parts of my life where I would let no one in. I watched one friend do things to others and not once did I think if she did it to someone else, then my turn may be next. I watched it happen to others, and I said nothing and did nothing about it. Guess what? My turn came, and I had to deal with the consequences all alone. I should not have made this person my friend because she did not reflect who I am as a person. Friendships are important because "no man is an island." We need each other. However, we need to choose our friends carefully.

Sometimes I felt discouraged or dissatisfied with my performance in school. Mama would always say, "Count your blessings." This meant for me to take hold of each day's blessings and cherish them with all my heart while looking forward to tomorrow's promises. Each day brings its own blessings. Be contented and grateful for what God has blessed me with.

Whenever someone gave me anything, Mama always reminded me and insisted that I say "Thank you." Sometimes a simple "thank you" is all it takes to warm the heart of someone else. I learned to be thankful and express gratitude for the smallest blessings I received because whoever bestowed those blessings upon me had a choice to withhold them from me.

When Mama got sick one day, she told me to help with her job, because her employer had to help her husband in the shop that day. I was very reluctant to go. I thought to myself, "Why should she care what those people had to do; it's none of her business? She was their maid. The pay was too small, anyway. She was always telling me to go to school and get an education, now she was sending me to do domestic work." It outraged me, and I became very belligerent. I thought to myself that this line of work was not for me. I couldn't figure out what was going on. I already had a pre-negative disposition to this line of work. Mama rebuked me harshly in a tone I had grown to despair, so I had to do as she told me. It turned out to be an excellent day. I got to see how the rich lived up close and personal. The kids liked me and wanted to be my friend. I was treated well. I did the same work I usually do at home, only this time I got paid. Not bad!

From this experience, I learned that there is dignity in every work. Whatever work I do, no matter how menial it may seem, I am contributing to the whole pie, and without my contribution, the structure may collapse. Always seek to be a valuable member of my team. I am never less than or better than anyone else. I am my own person, unique in every way. Always have a positive outlook in my demeanor and in everything I do. If I become a negative element, unlike Scientific Law that says, "a positive pole attracts a negative pole," much like a magnet. In the game of life this is different, negative elements attract each other. It's all in the attitude I present to the world and also my thought process.

There was a time in my young life when I was unsure about what I wanted to do when I grew up. Could I be a teacher, nurse, doctor, secretary or entrepreneur? My talents at this point were very diverse. After discussing this matter with Mama, she said, "You can do anything you want, just hurry up and make your mind up before it gets late. This here (as she made large downward circles with her right index finger) is not it." Somehow, I knew that she did not want ghetto life to be my destiny. She had high hopes and expectations for me. As an adult, this has a deeper meaning for me to be decisive. I knew what I wanted. I picked my path—decided and accepted the consequences of my choices. Sometimes I hit crossroads, and I made the adjustments through informed decisions, but I kept going. "Never give up," as Mama said. I was not afraid to make bold moves, seize opportunities, take enormous risks and capture the moment to enhance or improve my life. I learned valuable lessons from each move and was never afraid to ask for help when I needed it. In this world, there is no place for indecisions. If one cannot make up his/her mind, then a decision will be made for you. You may not like it, but you may have to live with it.

After I left nursing school, it was hard to find a job. I expressed my frustrations to Mama. She took my certificates and showed them to everyone she thought could help me obtain a job. They all promised to help. However, I was very impatient, and I left my hometown for what I thought was a brighter future. •

My lesson here was to be patient but persistent and make wise decisions in my determination. Keep knocking on doors until I find an open one. Sometimes it may seem long and hard but "do not give up" as Mama always said. Stay the course and be focused. If the salmon would quit swimming upstream, they would never get to their destination. I remembered when Mama wanted to form a group for her housing scheme; she talked to everyone whom she thought needed homeownership. Mama got many rejections and insults, but she kept on going, then she approached several

Ministers in the government and pitched her ideas until she found someone willing to help. She knocked on many doors and never gave up. She was patient and persistent. It took about four to five years from the time she conceived the idea until they built the houses, but she stayed the course and got what she wanted—to take her family out of the ghetto and into her own home.

Whenever someone came to visit us, Mama would always give them something to eat. Even though we were poor, there was always extra food in the house. If they needed anything and she had it, she always gave it away without hesitation. Mama was very busy and worked long hours, but she found the time to bake and cook for her friends whenever they placed the food orders. She either stayed up late at night or got up earlier in the mornings to get her work done to meet deadlines, and she would enlist me to help. Sometimes her customers did not pay, and Mama would say, "Let them go, they will lose more than that. They can't come back." This was true because the dishonest customers never came back, and they even passed us in the streets without speaking to us. They treated us as though they never knew us.

I would like to go further and add my life experiences here because not everyone appreciated the help they receive. I do what I can, leave them alone, and keep on moving. I am not trying to waste my precious time on ingrates. When I started my catering and sewing businesses on the side, I took a nonrefundable down payment from my clients. I was not trying to be defrauded. This experience has also taught me time-management and planning skills. Also, I learned not everyone can be trusted.

Whenever someone was speaking to Mama, I noticed that she always listened and seldom interrupted them. Somehow, she knew when a person was being untrue or would transmit incorrect information or as she expressed "deceitful." She warned about a person who talked too much or was always talking about someone or always knows what is going on in other people's lives. She emphasized that "They will talk about you behind your back too." And "You can't trust them." She even warned about the quiet person and said, "Still waters run deep." She hated gossiping and had no tolerance for it. I dislike gossiping too. There is nothing tangible to gain through gossiping. I have always felt that what's going on in my life was far more interesting than what's going on in another person's life. From this observation, I learned to keep friends and acquaintances that would enhance my life and choose my friends wisely. Also, to listen actively and observe body language before I speak or give my opinion. Often, the information that was being conveyed had a deeper meaning than what was being said, or the person may have ulterior motives. I also learned this through my life experiences.

Money was one of the greatest issues for us. Mama gave me money to save in my tin-cans and in the School Thrift Society. She always said, "Save your money for a rainy day." This worked for both of us. There were countless rainy days in our lives together. Somehow, Mama got us through them. I transferred this thriftiness into my adulthood and have reaped the benefits of a saved dollar.

Even though my grandmother was kind and nurturing, she was a very strong disciplinarian to her core. She believed that "children should be seen and not heard." She abhorred being disrespected and hated the destruction of her property. For example, some of my younger siblings were free-spirited. Mama would refer to them as "rude," "obstinate," "unmannerly," "disobedient," "rebels." She would yell at them whenever they were doing something contrary to her beliefs and disposition. It was very disconcerting to think a grandmother would use such descriptive words when referring to her grandchildren. To this day, I do not know whether she loved them. She never expressed her love for me, nor did she ever refer to me negatively. However, she was kind to my siblings when they were compliant or "obedient" as she said. During these times she played with them. I got the best of her. If I can remember, the word "love" was never expressed in my home or surroundings. I guess it's cultural, I do not know. However, I think she loved us all, judging by the things she did for us as children and adults. I have never heard the words "I love you" from my mother.

My lesson from this experience is that good communication is the key. How I communicate with another person is very important. It's not just what I say that matters, it's my tone, body language, appropriateness of what I say, and a whole myriad of expressions. If I care about another person, then I should attempt to make it known through good communication styles regardless of the situation. Also, I need to respect other people and their property regardless of how I feel about them.

Mama believed in God. She taught me how to pray when I was a child and made sure I said my prayers before I went to bed at night. She made sure I went to church every Sunday, even though she only went to church occasionally. She told the story about when she worked in Watooka. Every month she sent money home to a deacon in her church to make contributions on her behalf. She wanted to support her church. After working for several years, she returned home. When she went to her church and introduced herself to the new pastor, he did not know who she was. She then told him she sent her offering every month to Brother James to give it to the church. When Pastor Matthews and the treasurer checked, there was no record of her offerings. Mama said, "That man thief my money." Every time she saw him or heard of his name, she referred to him as "a scamp," "scampish," "no damn good and he calls himself a deacon," or "damn thief." She never spoke to him again. Whenever he met her in the streets and hailed out to her, she turned the other way and did not answer him. She never even talked to him in church. He never apologized, and I do not think she ever forgave him. She told this story quite a few times and whenever she was finished, she said "You can't trust everybody," or "You can't trust some people." The lesson here was don't trust everyone with your money. Be wise in parting with your money.

Mama got sick, and could hardly walk because of pain in her knees. She was diagnosed with rheumatoid arthritis. I invited her to my church so that my pastor could pray for her. She said she was not going. I was surprised and wanted to know why she was so adamant and determined not to get healed. So, I asked her. What she said next was a shocker. She said, "I will let him pray for me when he heals his wife." I said, "That has nothing to do with you that's their personal problem, just have faith that

God will heal you." She shook her head from side to side and said, "No, when he heals his wife." There are many lessons to learn here. Christians seem to be under a microscope unfairly, especially the leaders. Mama did not know if he was praying and trusting God for his wife's healing. As a Christian, I should be careful how I conduct myself because I may be hindering someone else. I should not judge another person, because I may not know what that person is going through. It's unfortunate, but some people look up to Christians for an example of "perfect living." A Christian cannot heal anyone. It is our faith in Jesus that heals. I should not allow anyone to be a hinderance when I am in need of prayer or anything.

After a while, I stopped listening to my aunt because she was always very controversial. Most times, I heard Mama yelling at her saying, "Why you always think about the worst thing?" or "Don't bother me, think 'bout something good." Somehow, I knew that she was telling Mama something negative about me. I think my grandmother was on to something here because our thoughts make us who we are and ultimately dictate what we do and how we live our lives.

"The dog who brings a bone always takes it back." This was a popular saying for Mama. She never listened to gossip; she stopped the person right in the middle of their sentence and let them know that she was not interested. Whenever that person left, she always said, "If I tell her something, she will carry it back." This is true. Sometimes what we say is used as a reference when others want to cause confusion.

"Don't put off for tomorrow what you can do today. Tomorrow never comes and is promised to no one." Mama never liked to hear me say, "I will do it tomorrow." The lesson here was "do not procrastinate." You may never have the time to do something you need to do, or opportunities may pass you by when you put things off. Something may hinder you at another time while trying to accomplish your task.

"Beat the iron while it's hot." Take advantage of every opportunity when it presents itself. You may never get the same opportunity twice.

"Don't curse the bridge before you cross it." I think this meant that you should not be negative before you know all the facts of the potential situation. Don't criticize anything before you have an opportunity to experience it.

"Make hay while the sun shines." Work diligently while you still have the opportunity. Or make the most of the opportunity while you still have the time.

"The longest road has an end." As a child, I thought it meant a physical road. Many times, I tried to imagine which roads were the longest and where they ended. In reality, it means that everything in life and every situation or circumstance has an endpoint or an expiry date. We may not like the ultimate results, but it must end at some point. Nothing lasts forever. Even gold can lose its luster, thus bringing about a change. As long as the earth keeps revolving, we will have changes. Before we can achieve a change, one period or phase must end before the other begins.

"Behind every dark cloud, there is a silver lining." Believe in hope. It may be difficult while you are going through the struggles of this life. But have faith; better days are ahead.

I remembered going home in excitement and telling Mama about a dress I had seen someone wearing. I told her I would buy the material and make the dress. It was a beautiful, A-line dress with fancy puffed sleeves. Mama rolled her eyes, turned her head from side to side and said, "Monkey see, Monkey do." This daunted my spirit, and I felt dejected. I left it alone. I decided that I would not act like a monkey. Lesson learned, don't follow anyone blindly, or be yourself and not try to be like anyone else. It could also mean to be authentic and not try to be like someone else.

"Parents eat sour grapes, children's teeth set and edge." I heard Mama talking to her friends. I never knew what it meant as a child. I believe it meant that children adopt their parents' habits and attitudes, which may not work to their benefit. Or, whatever the parents do, the children may suffer the consequences depending on the situation. Hence, the saying, "the sins of the parents fall on the children."

I loved to eat fruit as a child. Fruits were in abundance. It appeared everyone had fruit trees in their yards. Most times we (my classmates and me) just climbed the trees and picked the fruit without permission when we knew that the owners were not at home, were too old to run after us, or no one was living in the house. One afternoon, we planned to pick some mangoes, wash and peel them, then put salt and pepper on them and have a feast after school. On this day this activity did not work as planned. The boys climbed the tree, and the girls stayed at the bottom to collect the green mangoes. Suddenly the owner came home and caught us. We ran as though we were sprinters in an athletic event. The following day, Mr. Peters went to our school to complain to the principal. It was easy to identify students. Each school had a different uniform. Mr. Rollins, the principal, announced to the school what had happened the previous afternoon. He asked the students to tell the truth and come forward. Stanley promptly got up and identified each of us. This was very embarrassing. We were spanked in front of the school and told never to steal again. When Mama came home that night, she asked me what happened in school. I dared not tell a lie on top of stealing, when she already heard what happened. I related to her the entire truth. I thought I would be spanked again. Mama just rolled her eyes, looked at me and said, "When you go to thief, thief alone." This is all she said. I couldn't believe what I was hearing! So, was it alright to steal? Or whenever I steal, I must do it alone? Now I'm confused. I never picked fruits without permission again. This was no fun. The fun was in stealing the fruit and then getting away with it. Yes, I had a wicked streak in me!

"You can lead a horse to the well, but you can't make him drink." These words were real even as an adult. I tried in vain to encourage my younger sisters to study and do their homework. They often said, "I am not a bookworm." Whenever I complained to Mama that they were not doing their schoolwork, she always used these words. You can always encourage friends or loved ones, but you cannot make them do what they do not want to do. This brings me to the following statement:

"When you are coming up, bring someone with you." This has been an integral part of my life's journey. As a child, I shared with other children in need and helped in any way I could. As a young lady, I joined the youth group in our church. Every Saturday afternoon, we visited the elderly homes to help them with whatever they needed. We cleaned their homes, did the laundry and the shopping. As an adult, I continued to help wherever my services and expertise were needed, whether it was tutoring or counseling sessions with my students early in the mornings before school, during lunch or after school, I was there for my students, or just about anyone who needed help. I worked with several charitable organizations. The whole idea is to lift someone in need and be kind to each other. The key is, "don't be selfish."

"Hand wash hand, make hands come clean." Mama always encouraged me to help whenever I can. In helping someone in need, I may reap the benefits when I need help myself. Or, if I helped someone, they may return the favor.

I remember when a lot of emphasis was placed on establishing the role of women as the country was moving towards a more socialist and progressive agenda. Women were encouraged to come out of the shadows and kitchens to play an integral part in helping the young country succeed. A women's group was formed called the Women's Revolutionary Socialist Movement (WRSM). One evening my aunt came home laughing and telling the joke about one of her friends who was elevated to a high position in this movement and did not have the qualifications. "She can't even read properly what she gon tell people." Mama laughed and said, "Them putting square pegs in round holes." Lesson learned, it is unethical and could be dangerous and embarrassing to accept a position in which you are not qualified.

"You reap what you sow." A powerful and well-known statement. We cannot expect to reap a bountiful harvest when we have not put in the effort. You cannot expect to be successful if you did not prepare for success. Preparation is the key. This statement could also be applied in different situations especially in the decisions we make. We may have to live with the decisions we make.

After high school, I directed my search for a clerical or secretarial job since my qualifications met this type of work requirements. When Mama came home from work in the evenings, I usually told her what I was doing. Sometimes I got frustrated when I did not get a response. She said to me, "Don't put all your eggs in one basket." This meant that I should cast a wider net for my job search and look for other areas of opportunities. I did, and I got recruited by the nursing school.

Respect was high on Mama's list of priorities. She insisted that I say the magic words. "please, thank you, yes sir and yes ma'am." If the person is older than me, she always said to put a handle on their names. Example, Mr. Collins, Ms. Collins, Cousin Janet, Aunt Jane and so on. She went on further to say, "You are not playmates." This means that you are not in the same age group and I must respect my elders.

"As you make your bed, so shall you lie in it." I have heard Mama saying this many times, especially when I got into trouble. I guess it meant that I will have to live with the decisions I made.

"If rain ain't full it dew can't full it." Mama always said this to me when I was trying to do some last-minute studying before I went to school to take a test. I guess she meant that if I did not get it after studying for one hour the previous night, then I would not get it in five minutes. However, I found that a brief minute or two of review helped to refresh my mind.

"It takes one to know one." Even though Mama said this often. I do not believe this statement in its entirety. For example, one does not have to be a crook to know a crook.

"Do so, never like so." Mama often repeated this statement. I guess what Mama meant was, some people have no problem being unkind to others in words or in actions. However, they become angry when others do the same things to them. I believe, this is the same when she said, "Dem can give it, but dem can't take it." Lesson learned, treat others the same way you would like to be treated.

Even though my grandmother did not have a high school diploma or a college degree, her wisdom was superior. The advice she gave was not new or created by her in every case. However, she brilliantly applied them at the appropriate time. She learned from the school of life and experience. I thank God for placing such a prominent figure in my life.

Beginning Life After High School

*I waited anxiously, so long for this moment.
I worked hard and prepared for this day, my whole life. I
wished I had a future glass to investigate, so that I could
change parts of my colorful paths on the canvas of my life.*

Dr. Ingrid J. Benjamin Ph.D.

My high school days were now over. I had prepared for this day my entire life. What was a girl supposed to do? I did not want to go to college right after leaving high school. Anyway, I was too young to get employed. I was sixteen years old. I had to be eighteen to get a job. Sometimes, if you are lucky, you will get employed if you are younger. I wanted to work and help my grandmother have a more comfortable life after moving out of the ghetto.

Guyana was now a Socialist Country. Jobs were hard to find. Mama forced me to join the Young Socialist Movement (YSM) to get a job. My primary school teacher Mrs. Gordon assisted me in writing application letters and preparing a resume. They accepted me into Nursing School. My stay here was short, because I got sick and missed too many days of instruction, so I had to leave. They invited me to return the following year. However, I did not return because I had no desire or patience to wait so long to work. Education was now free. The government took control of all the schools both private and public. Secondary schools and colleges and the University of Guyana were also free. Nursing School was free too. They gave students a grant/stipend to attend.

My eighteenth birthday was approaching and since I could not find another job in my hometown, I went in total trepidation to my mother's house to find a job in the Bauxite Industry. As soon as I arrived, my mother pointed me toward Watooka to get a job as a domestic servant as she, my aunt and my grandmother had done. I told her I wanted to work in the office as a Stenographer (Shorthand-Typist). She gave me a very indignant look. Later, I heard her telling my younger sister that I think I am too good to do housework in Watooka, and they had a delightful laugh at my expense. She continued to berate me in front of my siblings often.

When my stepfather came home one evening, I asked him to help me since I did not know how to find a job with the Bauxite Company. He was a Foreman in the Company. We had an intelligent discussion about my qualifications, which included:

- Pitman Elementary, Intermediate and Advanced Typewriting and English
- Pitman Theory Stage One and Two–Shorthand. 120 Words Per
- Minute Shorthand
- Pitman ninety-two words per minute Typewriting.
- I also had several subjects at the General Certificate Examination (GCE) equivalent to the USA's high school diploma.

My stepfather was very impressed with my accomplishments and he promised to help me. Meanwhile, I did not tell my mother about my qualifications because of her negativity towards me. The following day he went to the office and set up an appointment for me. A few days later, I took a Typing and English test and passed with "flying colors." Within two weeks, they called me to work as a typist temporarily for six weeks. I put all my effort into it, and I worked conscientiously. Everyone was sad to see me leave. The supervisor promised to recommend me for permanent employment. However, there were no permanent positions available in that department. They called me several times to do temporary work in other departments. This continued for several months.

Working as a Typist in the Bauxite Industry (GUYMINE)

Meanwhile, I remained very unhappy at my mother's house. My living conditions there were by far too difficult and embarrassing to mention. For instance, my mother gave me rags, called bedding, to sleep on the floor under a window. It wasn't sealed properly, so the chilly night air seeped in under the window. I caught a terrible cold. When I coughed, you would think it was thunder roaring. My mother made a concoction and gave me to drink. It tasted so bad, but I had to drink it. She also gave me a Saab to rub on my chest and under my nose. This burned so badly, and the smell was noxious. I did not know what to do. I had no other choice but to use everything she gave me. By this time, my sputum was green. After a few days, the phlegm on my chest loosened, and I felt better. I guess the concoction was working. When my stepfather saw that I was sleeping on the floor, he said to my mother, "Let the boys sleep on the floor and give Ingrid the bed." My mother hissed her teeth and walked away. I remained sleeping on the floor under the window. There were so many instances of abuse; I find it difficult to transcribe.

The environment here had grown more toxic than when I was a child. I knew that I was unwelcomed here. I attended Calvary Temple Assemblies of God Church, where I met granddad. We became friends. He introduced me to his family who accepted me as a member of their family. He told me I could go to his home whenever I needed to relax. I took full advantage of this invitation and felt good doing it. The church was the only place where I found love, comfort and solace. I told no one in church what I was going through at home. I was too embarrassed. I only talked with granddad. Granddad took a special interest in me and made sure that I attended church regularly. He took me to church every Sunday, Wednesday and Friday. In the evenings after church, I walked home with Owen and Lennox. I enjoyed being with my peers at Christ Ambassadors every Sunday evening.

On Saturday afternoons we used to go to the mines and help the senior citizens with house-keeping and shopping.

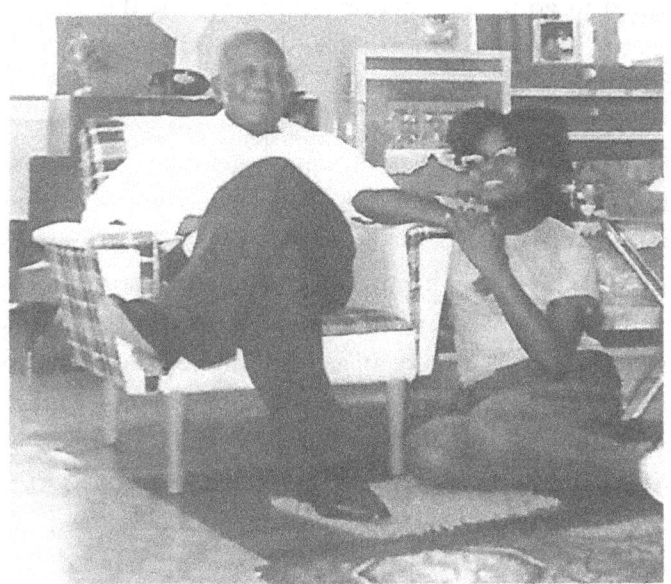

Granddad and me in his home

After several months, perhaps about a year, of working part-time and waiting for permanent employment, I got tired. I just had to get out of my mother's house. I heard that the Catholic Church would help with employment. I presented myself to the Catholic Church in Georgetown and asked them to help me find an assistant teaching position in the interior region of the country. I met with Father O'Connor, a very tall and burly white man. It almost scared me to death. I told him the reason for my request. He gave me a chance and hired me. He assured me that everything would be alright and that there were teachers who were already living there. He explained the entire process to me in a very calm and confident manner. When he was finished, I felt excited to take the plunge into an unknown and uncertain world.

The school year began in September and the Catholic Church helped me to get packed with a stipend and groceries to last for the entire semester (three months). My assignment was on the Pakaraima Mountains to live and work with the Amerindians who were the indigenous people of

Guyana. These Amerindians were from the Patamona tribe. One may ask why I wanted to go to the Interior? The answer is, the church provided the living conditions and groceries. And I was desperate to move out of my mother's house.

The only means of transportation to get there was by airplane. I arrived in Georgetown the day before my trip. I was accommodated in the Catholic Convent on Lamaha Street. The Nuns were very kind to me, and they seemed very happy. They were curious to know why such a young and inexperienced person would want to go so far away from home to work in such a remote area, where there were no prospects for a successful future. There were no means for an ambitious young person to get a higher education. No means of entertainment; just nothing to look forward to. After talking with the nuns, I remembered the question Mama asked me, "Do you know what you are doing?" I took a long pause before I answered, because I did not know what I was doing, nor did I think about the consequences of my actions. I just had a flight response to get away from everything. My honest answer was "No."

The next morning, I boarded the airplane at Timehri Airport (now called Cheddi Jagan Airport) in Georgetown. I watched as the men packed tons of cargo onto the plane, and then the passengers were told to board the plane. It was a very large airplane. This was my first flight and one that was so memorable, I couldn't even get the noise out of my head for several days after this flight. As the plane was taxiing on the runway, I looked out of the window and all I could see were tall trees on one side and the airport on the other. As the plane lifted off the ground, I felt defiance and rage, but a sense of relief, as I thought I was leaving all of the abuse and dysfunction behind me. The airplane flew high into the clouds and bumped into the cumulonimbus clouds as it ascended into the sky. It was evident that it was going to rain. Since it was my first flight, I did not know what to expect. As the noisy plane kept rolling along in one direction, the clouds were moving in quite the opposite direction. The sea saw motion of the plane caused my ear to pop and hurt. As I looked around to the other passengers on the airplane, the grimace on their faces told a story of fear and trepidation.

When the plane touched down at Cato airstrip, the rain had stopped,
The clouds had rolled away and gave way to mostly blue skies above.
There were also a few cirrus clouds in the sky.
In the distance I saw the majestic Pakaraima Mountains.
The serene look of the mountains gave me a
peaceful vibe that was indescribable.

By the time we landed at Cato airstrip, the passengers breathed a sigh of relief. We left the airplane shaken but in one peace. Cato was buzzing with life and activities. Tons of people including teachers from other schools came out to the airplane. There were smiling faces and greetings everywhere. They removed the cargo and mail from the airplane. Everyone came to claim their mail and cargo. I noticed that most of the cargo was comprised of groceries along with fuel and household items.

When I got here, the older school children and some parents welcomed me. Somehow, they knew my name and came prepared to meet me. Later, I learned that Father O'Conner had radioed them ahead of time and had given them instructions to help me. There were several boxes with my name and new address written on them.

Father O'Connor had made arrangements for my supplies to be shipped on the same airplane with me. The young men picked up my luggage and placed them on their backs in a basket-like container. (I cannot remember the name of the basket.) We started a slow but constant trek up the mountains. This was a two to three-hour climb through the forest.

It was beautiful, and the air was fresh, crisp and cool. The lush green surroundings were so serene and welcoming. This scenery made me forget about my troubles and what I was leaving behind. I felt adventurous, as though I would conquer something that no one else had ever seen. The tall green trees provided a shade from the sun, which barely penetrated the forest to give us enough light to navigate the narrow tracks under our feet. There were no houses or streets on our way up the mountains, no cars, buses or motorized vehicles, not even an animal-drawn carriage. I wondered how my guides knew where to go to find their homes, or, as a matter of fact, find their way around with no navigation tools. Then, I realized, this was their home, their environment, and they used their God-given instincts to navigate this rough terrain and for survival. We walked on quietly, no one said anything. The only sounds were birds chirping in the trees and the occasional blowing of the wind, making the tall tree limbs sway back and forth as if they were saying, "Welcome, welcome, welcome." We also made footprints on the moist tracks as we walked. Suddenly, everyone stopped and gasped with fear as their eyes followed the fresh path of a large set of paws that crossed our pathway. The silence continued, but fear stepped in. They said something briefly in their language and started walking with increased speed. Guyana is known for its large animals. The paw prints might have been from a Jaguar; I do not know. I was too afraid to ask.

We might have walked for what seemed like hours. We came to a large opening in the middle of the forest. I saw several mud huts, large and small, scattered in a group. It was late in the afternoon. The residents emerged from their huts almost in unison with smiling faces as they waved to us. I returned the wave and kept on walking with my guides, who never stopped or said anything. I think that the villagers were expecting me. I felt welcomed.

They took me to a small, but well built, furnished one-bedroom house. There was no electricity and running water. I found a flashlight with batteries and lamps with kerosene oil along with a three-month supply of groceries and other supplies. We collected the rainwater in large drums outside the house and pipes led from the drums into the house, providing potable water for cooking, drinking, bathing and cleaning. The facilities (bathroom & toilet) were in the house. There was a little stream with very clear water running at the side of the mountain. After surveying my unfamiliar environment, I got unpacked, ate a snack and settled in for the evening.

My one-bedroom home on the Pakaraima Mountains.

One of the teachers sitting on the water tank that supplied the house with fresh rain water.

A narrow stream ran parallel to the back of the house.

In the distance lies a little hill where the clouds rolled over from time to time engulfing it.

The next morning when I opened my wooden windows, the smiling faces of parents and children greeted me on their way to church. The words "Good morning Ms. Benjamin" with an unfamiliar accent that I hadn't heard before, still brings a smile to my face. They knew who I was, and they were very polite. The aroma of tobacco filled the air. This was a familiar odor, Uncle Andy smoked cigarettes. When I looked around, there were lush, green tobacco plants growing under my window.

The school was on top of a hill. Imagine being on a mountain, and then climbing further up a hill on that mountain, right after crossing a little stream that was powered with crisp, clear and clean running water from a nearby natural waterfall. I now reached the top of the hill and found a little school with about forty bright-eyed students waiting, filled with anxiety to be taught. A little Catholic Church sat about one hundred yards away, all alone. From this hill, the view was breathtaking. I saw the entire village. There were no roads, cars, electricity, industrial buildings or any of the makings of a big city. It was as though the entire community sat in a dome and was surrounded by tall trees in the distance. This was my new home, one in which I would get acclimated to quickly, whether I liked it or not. No one would come to my rescue. The next plane was one week away. Welcome to adulthood and the choices I have made. I now remembered the phrase Mama used to me, "As you make your bed so shall you lay in it."

The students were adorable. They were very polite. They were very keen and observant as they hung on every word the teacher said. I was very glad that Mama insisted that I spoke "properly" and carried myself with dignity. These innocent beings depended on the teacher to show them the way and lead by precept and example. They even copied the way the teachers wrote on the chalkboard. They were eager to learn just about anything.

The Patamonas were a very peace-loving and kind people. I enjoyed working with them. I saw many unusual vegetation and flowers as I walked through the forest. There were tobacco plants growing outside of the only door of my house too. On a cool day, I walked in the clouds, in the mornings on my way to school. This experience was heavenly. I felt closer to God as I walked through the clouds and felt their cool embrace. Sometimes it took a good minute for the clouds to roll by. I felt as though God was blessing me with His exceptional presence.

I did not miss the bright lights and excitement of a busy city life; instead, I embraced the quiet and healthy lifestyle of my new home. After all, I had the moon, the stars and the clouds close to me. I felt as though heaven touched my soul. This was comforting.

The Patamonas were farmers. They were self-sufficient in that they produced their own food, made their own clothes, and homes. Instead of a regular bed they used hammocks made from the cotton which they grew and harvested. They made the thread (twine) from the cotton. They made their houses of mud and the thatched roof made from dried palm leaves. Some of their pots, dishes and some utensils were made of clay. Their clothes were handmade or given to them by the Catholic Church. The older men and women wore their traditional garments, while the younger men, women and children wore the modern clothes, such as pants, shirts and dresses. Some of their tools were also handmade. They used the bow and arrow for hunting, fishing and protection. The women did most of the farming, cooking and cleaning, while the men hunted and protected the women and children. It is an unusual sight to see the women carrying the farm produce on their backs while the men walked behind with only theirs bows and arrows for protection. The foods included cassava (yuca) bread. This is a flat, white, soft or crispy round bread made from ground cassava. Pepper Pot was made from boiling real cassava juice until it becomes a dark brown sauce, then the meat was added. The wine was called Pywari, also made from cassava. This drink could knock you out for days. I believe that this wine had a high proof alcoholic content. The Ferine (main dish) was also made from cassava. They also ate corn, fish and meat. They loved spearfishing. They salted and dried their excess meat and fish in the sun.

I remember, as a child, I saw Mama making several dishes with cassava. She boiled it and we ate it with butter. She fried the cassava. She cooked it along with other vegetables in soup or what we call "dry-food" with stewed fish. She also cooked Metage with cassava and other vegetables. Cassava was boiled and mashed with seasonings, made into balls and fried. Mama also grated the cassava to make porridge. She grated the cassava and made starch to put on our clothes. This is an extensive process. From this same cassava, she made cassava bread, quinches and cassareep. I guess Mama was the true personification of the quote, "when life gives you lemons you can make lemonade" and so on.

This area was close to the Brazilian border. The Takutu River separated Guyana from Brazil. In the dry season (between July and September) parts of the Takutu River dried up making it easy for us to walk over to Brazil. Some of the other teachers, villagers and myself made trips, especially on the weekends to the tiny village across the river in Brazil to do our shopping. We also traveled to other cities including Rio de Janeiro (Brasilia). There were no border patrols on the Guyana side of the Takutu. However, there was a little police station on the Brazilian border. They never stopped us; in fact, they were friendly. The Brazilians welcomed us. They used the Guyana currency because the exchange rate was higher. I spent about one year living and working among the Patamonas.

One day, the Minister of Regional Development, the Honorable Philip Duncan, who was an Amerindian, visited the village with his entourage. He heard my loud typewriter and came over to see me. While we were talking, he offered me the job to become his Confidential Secretary. However, I had to apply for this position and send my credentials to the Ministry of Regional Development for approval. I did so, and I was later appointed as Minister Duncan's Confidential Secretary. This clerical job was what I was training for my entire life. I later moved to the Rupununi District, another part of the interior to assume my position. There were other Amerindian tribes living in this area. This was described as flat land – more or less.

Lethem was a livelier community, and in some ways, I was reminded of my hometown. It was teeming with lots of government employees. Soldiers and policemen were stationed here. I even had some suitors, whose proposals I spurned because I thought they were hopeless players. Further, I was not clear what I wanted to do with my life.

Triumphs of a Little Girl

Hon. Minister Philip Duncan and me

This position was challenging but fun. I traveled by land, air and water. The mode of transportation included land rovers, foot, horseback riding and airplane. I saw parts of Guyana that most people never got the opportunity to see, for example, an aerial view of the majestic Kaieteur Fall which is one of the world's largest waterfall having only one drop, and other natural water falls. This was quite an experience. During my tenure here, I also met several Ministers of the Government and other V.I.P.s during conferences.

Horseback Riding

One mode of transportation in the Interior.
The background shows an Amerindian hut with thatched roof.

However, after almost two years of exploration, I was ready for a change. I did not see a sustainable future for myself in this position. This was a political position and therefore, not permanent and could not augment the lifestyle I wanted to live. I was very thankful for the opportunity and experience I received. I then asked for a transfer, accepted a lower position and went back to my hometown, New Amsterdam, to work at the Regional Development Office as a typist. As long as I was at home, I had the time to plan my life for the future.

I got bored with the everyday routine. I realized that there were no challenges in this position and no areas for growth and development. I felt that I could do more with my life. I was not required to use my God-given talents to be creative and be challenged and my brain was getting foggy. I decided after one year that I would head off to teachers' college in Georgetown to study Home Economics. I liked to cook and sew and entertain. I would be a home economics teacher. After spending **one year** working in my hometown, I applied and got accepted into Lilian Dewar College of Education for secondary school teachers.

Minister Philip Duncan

Dressed in his native clothing

My College Experience

After years of conflicts and struggling with who I was and what I wanted to become, I decided on a career. I wanted to become a home economics teacher. This was where my genuine passion was.
My long-term plan was to become an entrepreneur –
own a bakery and restaurant.

For I know the thoughts that I think toward you, says the Lord, thoughts of peace and not of evil to give you a future and a hope.
Jeremiah 29:11

Triumphs of a Little Girl

When I arrived at Lilian Dewar College of Education initially, I studied Integrated Science (Chemistry, Physics, and Biology). However, I wanted to study Home Economics. The Carnegie School of Home Economics building was under renovation and not expected to finish until about mid-semester. As a result, all of the home economics students were placed among the various disciplines in the college. I was placed in the Science major course. When it was time for me to leave, the Chemistry lecturer, Mrs. Hubbard, summoned me to her office. She told me that I was not going because she checked my records, and I was doing very well in my science courses; Further, there were not many black people in Science. I felt very sad and was very disappointed. It appeared I did not have a choice. Mrs. Hubbard had already made that decision for me. From her tone of voice, she sounded very determined to keep me in the science classes. I was taught not to argue and be disrespectful to adults, so I politely stayed, but my heart was aching inside.

Mrs. E. Hubbard
Chemistry Lecturer

Science was the best thing that could have happened to me. It opened many gates of opportunity to me. I got to travel and live in places that seemed impossible to me when I was growing up. I traveled the world, either as a faculty member or on vacation. The distant places that I have daydreamed of, or have seen in books, became my reality and I embraced it. In my travels, I have met people from all over the world. I have taught some amazing students. I have worked with some incredible teachers. I have received many accolades for proficiency in the teaching of science. I also got Teacher of the Year Awards. Many of my scholars received awards in science and went on to study and work in Science-related fields.

Over the years, I have learned that Mrs. Hubbard was right. We need more people of color in the sciences. I am glad that I had accepted the challenge of teaching science. I never regretted it. Thank you, Mrs. Hubbard!

Student at Lilian Dewar College of Education

Three years came and went by very quickly. I met the most amazing students and lecturers at Lilian Dewar College. Most of the science students were focused even though we had so much fun. We helped each other as we formed study groups, shared lesson plans and students' aids whenever we were on student-teaching assignments. We had an artist in our group. Brian helped us draw our beautiful charts. The students loved them and were motivated whenever we used them. College was not just serious studies. We took a few trips together on weekends and holidays.

*Being in college made no difference to me;
I still liked to climb trees.*

Fun during a bush cook

Dr. Ingrid J. Benjamin Ph.D.

*"Bush cook" during one of our Holiday Trips Mr. Sankat,
our Biology lecturer joined us on this trip*

At this point, I must mention Mr. Oscar Sandiford. We fondly called him Sandy. Lilian Dewar College did not have dormitories. Some students stayed with relatives or friends in the city, while others commuted daily from their homes outside the city. Some students already lived in the city which made it easier for them. However, I was not fortunate to live with relatives. I tried, and it did not work out. I stayed at the Guyana Teachers' Association dorm. I spent just over a year here. The male teachers wanted to use the dorms whenever they had to conduct Union business in the city. I now had nowhere to go. I was in danger of quitting college. At this point, I did not know what to do. I told Sandy what was happening. He said to me, "You are not going to quit college; you will stay here and finish what you started." I was shocked. I felt like the luckiest girl in the world. Sandy was the caretaker for the building. He was a widower and lived at the back of the dorm in a three-bedroom apartment with his two children, Owen and Jenny. He told me I could move in with them. The first thing I thought about was, "How is this going to work?" since he did not have any extra rooms. To my surprise, Sandy gave me his bedroom while he moved to his living room and slept on a portable cot.

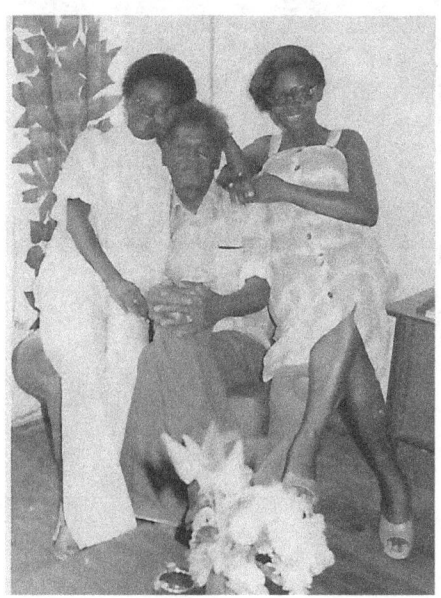

Jenny, Sandy and Me
Sandy made my dress and I tie-dyed it.

At nights he used a fold-out cot to sleep on. He did all the cooking and cleaning. Uncle Andy always made sure that I gave Sandy an adequate amount of money for staying in his home. Sandy never charged me a specific amount of money for room and board. Sandy also sewed men's and women's clothing. He even sewed for me, because college took up most of my time, so I had no time left to sew for myself. He once made me a "bad" cat suit and then warned me about wearing it out in public. I mean, what was the point? I just had to wear it. I must admit, I know I looked good in my cat suit!

Natasha and Me
I must say, my cat suit that Sandy made looks good.
I made Natasha's dress.
Mama's house is in the background.

I finished my college education unhindered and successful. I received a Trained Teacher's Certificate in Education, specializing in Integrated Science (Chemistry, Physics, and Biology), one year after college, as was the custom. Students did not receive their certificates until they applied for it one year after they left college. This was equivalent to an Associate Degree in the U.S.A.

I thanked Sandy for rescuing me. I am eternally grateful to God for placing such a kindhearted and considerate human being in my life. After college, I kept in touch with him, even throughout my journeys across the world. Whenever I went to Guyana, I always went to visit Sandy first before I went anywhere else. Sandy became the father I never knew. We talked about everything, including boyfriend issues. He always gave me his opinion whether or not I asked for it. He was very frank and did not fail to let me know when he thought my behavior was unacceptable. He treated me like one of his children. The one regret I had was that I could not go home to Guyana for his funeral, because of circumstances beyond my control. I grieved his passing quietly for a long time. Jenny told me that when he passed away, among the items that were found on his body, was my name, address and phone number. This was comforting because it reassured me that he accepted me, not as a stranger, but as a member of his family.

Finally, the time came for us to leave college. Three years went by so quickly. Somehow, we knew that we might not see each other again. We did not have a graduation ceremony as was the custom. Instead, we had an award or closing ceremony. Some students were given awards that they earned during their tenure in college. At this point, no one knew who had passed or failed the final exam. We were all unsure of our future as teachers. We said our last goodbyes and departed in different directions for our homes. It was sad to see everyone leave after such an incredible time together. The one regret I had was that we did not exchange addresses to keep in touch. I am thankful for Facebook; we are now trying to catch up after several years. As was the custom then, the students had to wait a few weeks for the results of our final exams. We were not given personal notifications of the results. Instead, the results were published in the newspapers.

The names of students who passed were listed alphabetically and by the disciplines we studied. We were later given individual notices as to our schools' assignments. According to our contract, we were required to serve our country for four years after college. Also, we had to accept teaching assignments anywhere in the country where there was a need for teachers. We did not have a choice of schools.

We all passed our exams and were sent to different schools across the country. I was assigned to Wismar-Christiansburg Multilateral High School in Wismar. This was a mining area. Bauxite and alumina were produced here. I previously lived in this area with my mother, but across the Demerara river on the Linden side. I was now living in Wismar.

The Multilateral High Schools were new and presented a different curriculum from the traditional high schools. They were focused on various disciplines such as science, the arts, and just about every career that a student would like to pursue when he/she left school. Wismar Multi, as it was fondly called, provided housing for teachers who came from out of town.

When school reopened in September, the new teachers were not paid or given a stipend until about two to three months later. I was very blessed to have Uncle Andy there for me again. Every Friday afternoon, he climbed up Blueberry and Chumbley Hills to bring me a week's worth of ration and money. He even told me to give Diane, another batch mate from college, some food. We shared the same apartment. This helped us out very well. In turn, I made bread and cakes every Saturday and took some for him. He was my guardian angel. But, Lord… he guarded me like a hawk! He was worse than Mama. I was warned about every man that came my way. I do not know how he found out, but he did, and I was sure to know it during his weekly visits. He knew who talked to me and for how long. I guess men gossip too. Not to mention, but he was a womanizer himself. He was not married, and he let his women know that he had to take care of his mother and was not going to get married until she died. Well, Mama died and he never got married. I could hardly remember seeing the same woman at his house twice. I guess he couldn't make up his mind whom he wanted to marry or maybe that was the lifestyle he wanted to live.

I served my four-years-contract, working at the Multilateral High Schools in Wismar and then in New Amsterdam, my hometown. I later resigned my position as Science Teacher and headed for the Caribbean. This was the beginning of my incredible journey around the world.

Triumphs of a Little Girl

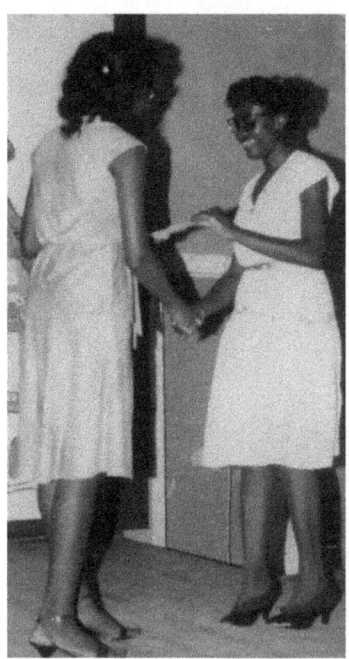

Receiving one of many certificates after college

Since I could not study Home Economics in college, and I still had a passion for cooking, baking, sewing and entertaining, I attended several extra-mural classes sponsored by the University of Guyana, after college. These classes included Cake Decorating, Sewing, Catering, Cooking, Baking and Arts and Crafts. I also sold cakes, pastries and cookies and catered for parties. The entrepreneurial passion was still burning inside me. This gave me some satisfaction. I was still doing what I loved and, in some ways, following in Mama's footsteps.

The Death Of My Stepfather

When Uncle Freddie died, it beckoned a new era for my younger siblings. This fragile family structure was now cemented in uncertainty.

At this point, I must interject and mention the death of my stepfather and the circumstances after that. My mother left him and moved to New Amsterdam with my grandmother, on account of years of his infidelity, verbal and physical abuse. Sometime after, my stepfather became ill and was hospitalized for a short while, and then he passed away. When I heard what happened, I crossed the river and went to my mother and asked her how I could help. She said to me and I quote, "I was alone in my marriage, and I will be alone in death." I guess this meant for me to back off and leave her alone. If she meant it literally, then I was only a child when she got married. It was her responsibility to take me to her wedding if she desired.

I did not know when his funeral took place and therefore, could not attend the wake or funeral. One of my younger sisters attended the same school where I worked. She suddenly disappeared and did not attend school. She did not visit me as usual after school. I missed her, so I went home to see what happened. No one was at home. I did this a few times with the same result. Later, I learned my mother took my younger siblings with her to live in New Amsterdam. Even after this rejection, I still offered her money to help out with the children because many were still very young and in school. She willingly accepted my contributions even after she received a lump sum of money from the Bauxite Company. I did not mind because I wanted to help.

Several months later, when I returned home to New Amsterdam, I discovered that my younger siblings were all placed in the wrong schools, except for my youngest brother. I promptly asked my mother to give me their birth certificates and school information so that I could take them to the Ministry of Education and have them placed in the correct schools and classes. Further, I asked her for her information so that I could get a relief from paying high taxes, since I was helping her financially. She did not answer me. I asked her several times and did not get a response. Finally, I told Mama what happened. Mama then told me what she said, and I quote, "I do not want anybody to hamper me and my children." Now, my mother was a very superstitious person. She believed that if she gave me her and her children's personal birth information that I would harm them through witchcraft. After this discussion with my grandmother,

I became very confused, and I could not believe what I was hearing. The thought of hurting anyone was inconceivable to me. Once again, I was dumbfounded; I could not find words for a response. I was in a state of shock. I had never sought the services of a witchcraft worker in all of my life. I had never done witchcraft. I did not know what she was talking about. Those thoughts never came to my mind. I wondered why I would want to hurt young children who were my siblings. Why would I want to hurt my mother? I did not even know where to go to find witchcraft. Besides, I was a Christian, and I had accepted Christ as my Lord and Savior. I was also a Sunday school teacher. Why was this happening? I broke down in tears and stared at the walls and ceilings for what seemed like hours. Once again, my mother rejected me.

When I could gather myself together and think about my relationship with my mother, I realized that it was nonexistent and that I was forcing myself upon her and her children. I needed to leave this alone and get on with my own life.

I taught science in the same high school where my youngest brother attended. Whenever I saw him in the hallway, I was afraid to speak to him, so I just smiled and kept on moving. Many times, when I saw him, his clothing especially his pants were not fitting him well. Somehow, I knew his mother had made them for him. It ached my heart. I wanted to purchase some school clothes. Once again, I was afraid so I left it alone. To this day I do not have an amiable relationship with my mother and siblings except one, Carol. You see, Carol and I are kindred souls, born under the same circumstances and suffered in similar ways. We are very close. However, if my siblings acknowledged me, I would never reject them.

In 2014, after twenty-plus years of being incommunicado, I thought this estrangement had to end. I decided that we should at least come together and have a family reunion. Everyone had families of their own and lived in different parts of the world. Further, the children did not know all of their cousins and aunts and uncles. I also thought that we could send gifts and cards to each other, especially to the children on their birthdays and holidays. Obviously, we had to know each other's birthdays for this to work. I had completely forgotten about the prior incident when I tried to help my siblings. This was the worse idea I had. I did not get a response from most of my siblings. My mother sent me her information, which stated that she was born in the nineteen-thirties. No specific day, month or year was mentioned.

I thought since everyone was grown and moved away from home, and lived among other cultures, that their thought process would have evolved into a more forward-thinking, progressive manner. It appeared time had stood still. I eventually canceled the reunion. At this point, it was evident to me that some of my siblings were not interested in reconciliation or any form of association with me. I just wonder what the thought process was. I have been there for all of my siblings, even though some were too young to recognize it and I have been rejected time and time again by our mother. My older siblings have been the recipients of my generosity time and time again. When one of my sisters was very ill in Mackenzie hospital, I was there for her every day until she was transferred to Georgetown hospital. Even then I went in search of her, to help and to make sure that she was alright. I almost lost my job while I was taking care of her. She has been my fieriest critic after all I have done for her. It appears those negative feelings about my sister Carol and I have never dissipated and are still prevalent, even to where they still did not want to associate with us. I honestly do not know what we have done to leave such negative imprints on their hearts. After all these years, we were still treated as outcasts. I can go on and on, but I will leave it alone. This is an energy depleting activity.

However, my mother seemed to be willing to reconcile with her two "outside" children (Carol and me). She brought us food and snacks and even took pictures with us when we were home in the Summer of 2014. I had to return home to Guyana in 2015 on business. My mother came to visit me. She brought me fruits and spent a few hours with me. We chatted about the neighborhood, the latest in Guyanese politics, my life abroad, my near-death experience and just about any random thing that popped up. She told me she was praying for me and she knew I would recover and be alright. I thanked her for lifting me up in prayer when I needed it the most. When she was ready to leave, I stood at the front door to say good bye. She walked towards the gate, then suddenly turned back and came towards me. She gave me a hug and a kiss. Imagine my shock attack. I was left speechless. It only took her fifty-five plus years to get so close to me and express such positive emotions towards me. I just wondered if this was redemption or final acceptance. Either way, I will take it. I realize that I may never understand or even get answers to many questions that still linger on my mind. But life goes on—we'll see what happens. I am optimistic. There is still hope, and I do believe in possibilities. I am trusting God for an awesome outcome.

My Grandparents

This was an unbelievable union, between a man and a woman who were worlds apart, and totally incompatible. A union that was truly unbelievable and mind-boggling.

Dr. Ingrid J. Benjamin Ph.D.

My Grandparents' Wedding

This is the only picture I managed to salvage.
Mama destroyed the others.
I have never seen pictures of my mother and her
siblings when they were children.

My grandmother was a woman of few words. She can even be characterized as being very blunt or short with words. She never had much to say. However, sometimes she told me stories of her life with her parents and husband. Her stories always ended with "Mother have, father have, blessed is the child that has his own." She told the story of how her mother died of a heart attack on Christmas Eve while preparing for the family's Christmas festivities. Shortly after her mother's death, the family separated.

My grandmother was the fifth of seven children. The family lived in a village on the Corentyne which is in the country-side in the county of Berbice. Her father, Jim Barry, owned hundreds of acres of land, cattle and livestock. He was a wealthy farmer. He made sure that each of his children and their descendants gained a sizeable portion of land.

My grandmother was a dancer. Whenever she told stories about her dancing, she lit up with excitement. There was no doubt that she loved dancing. We could see the stars in her eyes and her body language told the rest of the story. She described her dancing as "on her toes and light on her feet." She had a rhythmic walking pattern that would make anyone take a second look as she passed by. Even in her old age, she sat with an erect posture and never sloughed. She won many awards for her excellent dancing. Her career choice was to become a teacher. This was not to be realized. The rule at that time was that a married or pregnant woman could not be a classroom teacher. I learned that this was the British rule.

A few months after the death of her mother, the family scattered in different directions. Mama went to Town - New Amsterdam in search of work. She met and married my grandfather, Walter Stewart. They were married on December 28, 1929. He was fifty years old, while she was only twenty-seven years old. He was, in my great grandfather's classification, "beneath her standard in every way." My grandfather, whom I was told I renamed "Dada" was a very short, poor and mixed decent man – black and white. These physical features were poor qualities, according to Jim Barry, my grandmother's father. This meant that mama was "spoiling the Barry breed." The Barry's were known to be very tall, dark, and strong and not to mention wealthy. She had now become an outcast. None of her siblings recognized her nor attended her wedding. When her father passed away, her oldest brother, Charles, was the executor of the will. He sold some property and distributed it among his siblings except for my grandmother. The only thing she got was two parcels of land—the front parcel to build a house while the back portion was to be used for farming. This was only because her name was on the deed. Mama never claimed this land.

My grandfather was a boat builder. After marrying mama, he took her to live in the ghetto, a tenement yard, with several little houses, similar to where I was raised. His mistress—the other woman—lived in one of those houses with his son Thomas in the same yard. He was my grandfather's oldest child.

This was the beginning of a long life of physical, verbal and mental abuse. There was no peace, joy or love in the home. Mama bore four children and was not given the opportunity to raise them with the same respect and dignity as she was raised. The other woman controlled her home. She told my grandfather how to run his home with the ultimate precision. He did exactly what she said. He did not even discipline his own children. They were allowed to do whatever they wanted. Meanwhile, his mistress ensured that mama had a horrible day, every day, while she often encouraged Dada to sleep with her on occasions. Life here was filled with sadness, cruelty and embarrassment. Mama told stories of him beating her, especially after he visited his mistress. Even when she was naked and pregnant, the beatings continued. She mentioned after beating her one day he kicked her in her private.

When I think about the stories Mama told me as a child, I often wonder about the condition of the human heart. How could anyone be so heartless? What was the purpose of the marriage in the first place? Why didn't he marry his mistress? He knew her before Mama. Why didn't mama just return home to the safety and comfort of her father's house? As a child, when I listened to these stories, I felt very sad, but I did not have the wisdom to ask these pertinent questions that are now burning in my heart. However, I perceive that she did not want me to suffer the same fate and agony as she did. She poured her soul into me and made the ultimate sacrifices so I would not follow in her or my mother's footsteps and make the same mistakes. She even talked about my mother making the same mistakes as she did, but with a few exceptions. My stepfather was not dirt poor, and he had a better job, also, I have never seen him hit her even though she accosted him at times. Everything else was "same old–same old."

My grandmother's siblings hardly visited her. In fact, her youngest brother, whom she helped to get his education while he attended trade school, lived in the same town, and he and his family never visited her. Not while I was growing up. He became a wealthy businessman. She, however, visited them occasionally. I remember as a child, Mama and I used to visit her brother. We often walked through the back door and took a seat in the kitchen where we were served drinks and cake. We were never invited into the living room. My great uncle had three wives and my grandmother was never invited to any of his weddings. My grandma and her family were also never invited to any family celebrations. To this day, I do not know most of my relatives. Those who I know are just mere acquaintances. There is no real family bond. Mama visited her relatives on the Corentyne sometimes. She always took me with her whenever she visited.

Mama left Dada after enduring years of abuse. The children were now grown and could survive on their own. She picked up herself and moved far away to Mackenzie alone. Knowing no one here, she become a live-in domestic servant. She did this for several years. Meanwhile, Dada continued to live in the ghetto with his children and mistress. He died when I was about three years old. I do not remember much about him. I can only remember playing tea-time with him on the floor. We played with my little teacup and saucer set.

Whenever Mama told me stories about her life, and what Dada did to her, she always ended with "Don't let any man take advantage of you." One story she told me that still causes me to chuckle is, "That man had ah old working pants. I sew and patch that pants til there was no place left to sew. There were patches on patches and holes on the patches. Then one day he was hallowing on me to patch that pants. I throw that pants in his face and tell him, I ain't sewing no damn bedding, (meaning old and tattered clothes) go buy a pant." She said that he just stood there and looked at her. This was the first time she acted in this manner. She said, "If he only tek God out of his thoughts and knock me again, I was gonna out his lights." as she waved her index finger in the air from left to right and shook her head angrily. I believe that at this point, she was sick and tired of years of battering and that she had rebelled because she had enough of his abuse.

My aunt told stories of herself and her older brother, Uncle Andy, fighting regularly. Whenever this happened, both of them did not go home after school. They went to Dada's work and waited on him, so they would go home together. Somehow, they knew that the children's parents would go home to complain to Mama, who would spank them upon receipt of this complaint. So, they didn't want to be hit, but it was okay for them to hit other children! My aunt always boasted with joy and laughter about the many fights she won as a child. Whenever she boasted about her conquests, Mama said to her, "This is a feather in yo cap." This meant sarcastically that this is a great accomplishment for her. However, my mother and her siblings had fond memories of their father who seemed to spoil them rotten. Regardless of the circumstances, he never disciplined them. After his death, Tita my aunt and uncle Urban went to live in Georgetown with their oldest brother Thomas. My mother stayed in New Amsterdam for a while, and then she went to join Mama in Mackenzie. Uncle Andy also moved to Mackenzie where he went to trade school, had an internship in the bauxite company and later permanent employment.

My Mentors

During this incredible journey that I have been blessed to experience, I have met the most amazing people of strength, honor and substance. God has made me in his own image, and these precious souls have taken this unknown seed, planted it and placed it on an open window. Here the warmth of the sunlight and the drops of rain have helped this seed germinate and grow into a wonderful tree.

I bow down to my mentors in gratitude and appreciation for their true love and friendship and for nurturing and holding me up while I stood on their shoulders. I am indeed the product of "A village." Thank you village.

Mama – Mrs. Pearl Stewart
My all-time champion. My Rock!

Uncle Andy - Picked up when Mama couldn't do it anymore.
Uncle Andy supported me at every stage of my life. Whether it was elementary, high school or college, he was there for me. Even after I left college and went to live and work in Wismar, he was always there for me.

Granddad - Walter Davis

I met granddad at Calvary Temple Assembly of God Church in Linden. He was a beacon of light, strength and support in my life. He encouraged me to be the best young lady I could be and hold on to my Christian values. He also encouraged me to enroll in Bible School. He made sure that I was at church every Sunday, Wednesday and Friday evening. Even though I was not his flesh and blood, he accepted me into his home. Even his wife and children accepted me and treated me as a member of the family.

I know that God put this beautiful relationship together. HE knew that I needed a friend and a helping hand at that time in my life.

Innar-Brother Rudolph Innocent

There is so much that I can say about Innar. He was the only person Mama trusted to take me out. He was a staunch Christian. We only went to church, though. He picked me up every Sunday afternoon to go to Christ Ambassadors Service in church. He did "his job" faithfully every week. He made sure that I was "delivered" back to my grandmother's house "safe and sound" after the evening service was over.

Sandy - Oscar Sandford

Sandy was my chief supporter during my college years. He was responsible for me completing college. I met him at the Guyana Teachers' Association dormitory. Sandy allowed nothing to bother him to the point of depression. As always, he was upbeat and happy. He made the best pumpkin fritters. He always used the term "I am God's own child."

Aunty Carmen – Camille Stewart

Aunty Carmen: Uncle Urban's wife: She introduced me to the world of cosmetics. I could not complete my holidays on the Essequibo Coast without a bag of cosmetics and a bag of new clothing. She taught me about puberty. She made the best fudge and tried to teach me to do the same. This was in vain. To this day, I still do not know how to make fudge.

Nen and Maudi–two of life's angels

Maudi lived with Nen in an apartment in Brooklyn, New York. They accepted me into their hearts and home when I moved to New York. I was introduced to them by Nen's niece Maria. They helped me get started with life in New York. They treated me like a member of the family.

Mrs. Era Henry

We fondly called her Gigi. I was introduced to her by her daughter Nettamae when I lived in Georgia. Our relationship blossomed into a beautiful friendship more like a mother and daughter. We joked about her adopting me. She cared about me deeply. She advised me when I needed help and direction. She was my prayer partner. She became my confidant as we shared secrets. Gigi went home to be with the Lord knowing that I will be alright. She was one of life's angels.

Mrs. Daphney Gordon: Mrs. Gordon was my elementary school teacher. She was very instrumental in helping me to find employment after high school. Even though I left elementary school, I still kept in touch with my teachers. She helped me to write my resume and letters of application and filling out application forms.

Mrs. Devry: Another of my elementary school teachers. She taught us needlecraft, and on some weekends, she invited me and another student to her home to help her prepare cakes and pastries for her guests.

Mrs. Tucker: She was not our classroom teacher. She was senior mistress and later deputy head mistress in our school. She was very instrumental in helping to prepare us whenever there were national exams. She tutored us after school from Monday to Friday. She even invited us into her home on Sunday afternoons for tutoring. She tutored us free.

Mr. Rampersaud: My high school chemistry teacher. He was very instrumental in preparing his students for exams. He tutored us in the afternoons after school, and on Saturday mornings free.

Mrs. Geneva Rutherford: My principal at Mary Star of the Sea School in the Bahamas. She willingly accepted the challenge of proctoring my exams while I was working on my Master's degree.

There were many other elementary and high school teachers who took an intimate interest in my well-being and went above and beyond the call of duty to help me succeed. Each mentor helped me at different stages of my life. I guess I became a teacher because of all the attention, interest, encouragement and mentoring I received from my teachers.

Gratitude should be a building block in our success process. Everyone we encounter in our lives would have built a bridge, which would lead us to success or failure. I always remember to give thanks, as Mama taught me, because there are lessons to be learned in success and failure. I try to endeavor to learn from each experience.

My Travels and Achievements Abroad

*"Have I not commanded you? Be strong and of good courage;
Do not be afraid, nor be dismayed, for the lord your
God is with you wherever you go." Joshua 1:9*

It was challenging to live and work in the Caribbean while traveling to the USA to study. So, I moved to the USA in pursuit of my educational goals. I headed to New York to work and study. This was the only alternative to achieve my goals. It was extremely demanding because I also brought my cousin Natasha who was fourteen years old with me. She had lived with me in the Caribbean since she was twelve years old. She is my aunt's daughter. After years of tormenting and bullying me, my aunt made peace with me and asked me to take care of her only child because she could not manage it by herself. As a matter of fact, when she was about to give birth, she asked me to take care of the baby if anything should happen to her. I accepted this responsibility. I also had to support Mama and my aunt who was taking care of her.

After we established ourselves, I went back to college. I worked as a science teacher during the day and went to college at night. I even picked up a few part-time jobs along the way to "make ends meet" as they say. For many years I worked hard and struggled through the adverse weather, including winter storms. I faced every challenging situation that presented itself, head-on.

Science Teacher

Even though I was under extreme pressure, I consistently encouraged my students to succeed, specifically those who were struggling and had academic challenges. I offered free tutoring early in the mornings before school, during lunch or in the afternoons after school. I conducted workshops to assist students with college and high school preparation. I facilitated Science Clubs and Science, Health and Career Fairs to support my students to have a rewarding experience in science and make informed decisions for their future. I planted trees with my students during Earth Day to make them aware of the importance of saving this planet. I even planted a garden with my students to allow them to experience how their food is grown. We made delicious dishes with our produce.

I have a passion for science, and I believe that every child can learn something in science because it is all around us. I approached the subject in my classroom with this same tenacity and energy while working with each student to motivate them to unfold their God-given potentials. Many of my students received science awards and accolades for their hard work. I sought to give back what was given liberally to me when I was a student.

To date, the positions I held in academia at different times during my journey are summarized as follows:

- Stenographer, Confidential Secretary, Typist,
- Assistant Teacher, Science Teacher (Physics, Chemistry, Environmental Science, Integrated/General Science) Health Education and Math, Head of Science Department
- School Guidance Counselor, Director of Guidance
- Career Counselor for a Summer School program
- Dean of Studies, Associate Professor
- Substance Abuse Counselor
- Clinical Hypnotherapist Instructor and Life Coach.
- Founder and Director of the American Center for Self-Development.
- Curriculum Development

Some of my academic achievements and awards are:

- Associate Degree (Trained Teachers' Certificate) in Science.
- BS Degree (Honors) in Health Education

- MS Degree (Honors) in Education, specializing in School Counseling
- Ph.D. Degree (Magna Cum Laude) in Education Counseling
- Certificates in Advanced Clinical Hypnotherapy and Instruction
- Alcohol and Substance Abuse Certification
- Licenses in School Counseling and in Science
- Many certificates, recognition, and accolades in the teaching of science
- Teacher of the Year Award

Extra-curricular Activities and Volunteer work – at different times:

- Lion Club
- School Thrift Society Treasurer
- Brownie/Girl Guide–Scouts Leader
- Church – Sunday School Teacher, Secretary, Chairperson in the Education Dept.
- Science Club, Health Club and Craft Club Moderator
- Science and Health Fair–Judge and Moderator
- Career Fair Moderator
- Volunteer Counselor and Life Coach
- Before and after school tutor
- CASA -Court Appointed Special Advocate
- Developed a Teenage Pregnancy Prevention Program and Handbook for my high school students.

I am particularly proud but humbled and appreciative when I contemplate my humble beginnings and what I have accomplished despite my upbringing, despite my dysfunctional family and despite the putrid environment in which I was raised. My students' success rate in national Science and Health exams were between 97% to 100%. I remember working in a prestigious private school, where the students were placed in classes according to their abilities. The students in the "lower ranks" were not allowed to take national exams for fear they would cause the school's averages in each subject to decrease. If this happened, then the school would lose its prestigious position. These students were given a certificate of attendance at their graduation. When I learned of this situation, I told the principal that I would be registering all of my students to write the science and health exams. He said that science is a very difficult subject and they would never be able to make it. I told him I will work with them. I worked with my students every day after school for one hour. We did additional labs and science projects along with student teaching. I made science fun as I tried to hone in on each student's learning style to be able to reach them where they were in the learning process. Some of the other students became jealous and wanted to join us, so I made them work in groups and help other students. My plan worked. Most of my students passed. As a matter of fact, science topped the charts with 97% and health with 100% We had the highest percentage of any other subject. I was at home when the principal called to give me the good news and congratulated me.

As an educator, I also taught Health Education in high school. Almost every time I taught human reproduction, at least one young lady came up and asked why didn't I teach this before? I also observed that a few young ladies were entering high school pregnant. This was bothersome to me. Every year I devoted at least one class period to discuss life issues with my students because I know what life was like to grow up without responsible parents. I was astonished to learn that most of my pregnant students needed someone to love them. They thought pregnancy was the answer. Whether that love came from a boyfriend or a baby, it did not matter. They did not consider the responsibility and care of a newborn baby and a growing infant or a boyfriend who may or may not be present in the baby's life. Before a baby can express his or her love for anybody, quite a lot of work, time and energy must be invested into nurturing this baby. I later developed a Teenage Pregnancy Prevention Program to awaken students' awareness to the responsibilities of parenthood. I also encouraged young women to first love and respect themselves, appreciate and accept themselves before getting into a serious relationship with their boyfriends. I know this is not my place, but someone had to say it. Our precious young women needed a reality check.

To better support and motivate my students to study science, I moderated Science and Health Clubs after school. I worked with parents and leaders in the community to help students through sponsoring Career, Science and Health Fairs. Most students believed and even complained that science was too difficult, but they always rose to the occasion when they were motivated, encouraged and challenged.

Reflections On My Childhood And God's Amazing Grace

It is said that one cannot move forward while looking in the rear-view mirror. Sometimes the rear-view mirror can serve as a reminder as we struggle to find the right direction and make adjustments to life's meandering pathways. Keep moving forward. Living in the past would do you no good.

Triumphs of a Little Girl

When I think about my childhood, I wonder what I was thinking. I had no role models whom I would have liked to emulate entirely. There were, however, influential people in my community, including my teachers, whom I admired and dreamed that one day I would be as or even more successful than they were. Up to that point, no member of my immediate family had gone to high school or tried to advance their lives in any significant way, except for my uncles. Even though they did not go to high school, they could still find lucrative jobs. Uncle Urban went to a commercial school and later opened his own school. Uncle Andy went to a trade school, interned and became a mechanic. They did not live with us and only visited us occasionally. My mother and aunt were domestic servants. My mother later became a housewife. My aunt took a craft course in making cushions. She taught this course for a short while and soon abandoned it and went back to doing what she knew was more comfortable for her, which was domestic work. Later, she went to work harvesting sugar cane in the fields. The people in my immediate neighborhood did not go to high school. In fact, they did not even complete elementary school, and therefore, had no useful skills to make a worthwhile contribution to society. There was one man who was an exception. He had a government job while his wife, Ms. Angie, stayed at home and took care of the home and children. They only lived here for a short time.

However, there was an uncommon scenario across the street from us. There were large single-family houses, and the occupants did not associate with us. They were middle-class families, with careers. There was a teacher, an attorney, an engineer, and a land surveyor. I admired them and had a special fascination for their lifestyles, which seemed to encompass grandeur, dignity, and success. It's interesting to see how these two worlds coexisted on opposite sides of the same street but never commingled with each other.

Another factor I had to deal with while growing up was the color of my skin. I found out that being of African descent might not be the only socially qualifying factor for acceptance in some social circles. Rather, one's degree of blackness preempted acceptance or rejection. The terminology "Black is beautiful" was not true in every circumstance. For instance, whenever I heard the terms "She has nice skin," "She has a nice complexion," "She has nice hair," or "She has nice soft hair," I knew that this was not regarding me, because the admiring gaze was always on someone else. When I visited my hometown a few years ago, someone asked me: "So long as you are in America, you didn't get fair yet?" I did not answer this ridiculous question. I did not know that America can make someone have "light skin." I thought one's natural skin color was because of genetics. Although some of us bleach our skin, this was and is not my preference. I feel I am more than the color of my skin. My unblemished character and the way I lived my life is far more important. Believe me, there is a wealth of content and character here. Whenever someone made any disparaging remarks about my dark complexion (for example "blackie") my grandmother told me to ignore them and just continue doing what I was doing. They are not better than me. She also said I should not get angry, just ignore them. They are not worth my time. As a child, this advice was hard to adhere to. It often made me feel sad and embarrassed about my dark skin.

As a young woman, it did not affect my self-confidence, but it affected my personal and social identity to where I didn't dare to wear black or any dark clothing for fear it would make me appear to be darker than I was, and I wouldn't be attractive and no one would like me. This negative self-consciousness lasted throughout my pre-teen and teen years, coupled with the fact the opposite sex often told me I am not pretty, but I could "pass." I later realized that my physical appearance did not matter. My heart was in the right place. God made me this way—perfect in His image. That was Jehovah Makkeh— the Lord who molded me in His awesomeness made a masterpiece when I was molded! They were missing out on what might have been the best wife or friend they could have ever had. That was their loss. So, I held my head up high and continued on the road to success. God loves me and that's all that matters. I now wear my dark clothing with pride. I knew that I had no control over what others thought or said about me. I could only control my reaction, which was to "leave stupidity, arrogance, and ignorance alone." If they were too stupid and ignorant to understand or appreciate the basic concepts of genealogy and genetics, then they were not worth having me as a friend.

Triumphs of a Little Girl

As a child, no one told me how to study, be organized, be clean and neat, and work hard to become a successful woman. I just did these things on my own. No one told me about the importance of education. No one told me that there were rewards in having an excellent education. Somehow, I knew that education was the key to getting out of the ghetto. My grandmother only kept telling me not to allow any man to take advantage of me. I think in her own way she was telling me I should always strive to be independent, which would lead to my success. They never forced me to study or to get good grades. I learned the hard way that good grades were important and expected, regardless. I got the unspoken subliminal messages.

There was an incident once when I brought home my report card which had me ranked at number four in my class. I had dropped from number one. When I showed Mama my report card, she read it, then she got up, went to my bookshelf and yanked all of my Archie comic books down and said in a harsh tone, "This is rubbish." She threw all of my comic books away. In my mind, I was saying, "This woman is really crazy!" She never explained why she did it, and I was afraid to ask. I swear, this was the saddest day of my young life. I was about nine to ten years old. I loved reading comic books. I used to swap them with my friends and couldn't wait to get the next issue. I had so much fun. Now they were gone. I could no longer keep up with Archie and Veronica. Of course, I could have removed my comic books from the garbage when Mama went to work the following day, but I was afraid of getting caught. If this happened, I didn't know if I could deal with the consequences; so, I left it alone. Up to this point, Mama never spanked me. Every time I passed by the garbage, I checked to see if my prized possessions were still intact and to see if Mama had changed her mind and let me have them. I even covered them with a plastic bag to protect them from other garbage. That was a vain desire, as it never happened. Then, one day when I came home from school, the garage was empty. I knew that the Town Council had picked up the garbage along with my precious possessions. This was the end of my Archie comic days. If I were bored and needed something to read, I had to go to the library. We only had a few books at home which I got as gifts, and I had already read them. Somehow, I learned from this painful episode that good grades, also called marks, were important and that Mama would accept nothing less from me. It was my job to bring home a good report card. Again, that was the unspoken word and her way of telling me to do well in school.

After this incident, I became a "pain in the butt." When I wasn't sewing with Ms. Irene or helping Madam Thom, I helped Mama to cook and bake in the kitchen. When my aunt taught young women to make fancy cushions, I got right in the "thick of things," and learned how to make these cushions too. I also learned how to knit and crochet just about everything—bags, chair covers, centerpieces, table cloths, baby socks and more. I had to be kept busy. Even when Aunty Carmen came to visit, I used to ask her to show me how to make different kinds of fudge, peanut cakes/brittle and sugar cakes. No visitor could have escaped my curiosity. They had to share their talents and knowledge with me. I was totally unguarded and unfiltered.

I now turn my attention to the evil men in my life while growing up. When I think about the men who tried to assault me sexually, I have many questions. I wonder what force of nature propelled them to have such a heinous desire. Did they think sexual impropriety is the prelude to manhood? Was this a rite of passage for men? Did they think they had the absolute right to treat me like a doormat? As a child, I often heard the expression, "Women are the weaker sex." Again, I wonder if men felt that this was their passport to disrespect and violate women's bodies.

This behavior transcends across racial and ethnic groups and is a direct reflection of the condition of the human heart. My first attacker was black. The next one was White/Portuguese. The last one was of mixed descent, Black and Indian. Negative sexual behaviors also transcend age. My first two attackers were between the ages of sixteen and seventeen. The last one as it may seem to a child was ancient; he might have been in his forties or even older. We often hear the expression, "Dirty old men." However, I realize those dirty old men were once "dirty immature young men." As my grandmother always said, "A leopard never loses its spots." These expressions of disgust and disdain were not meant to discredit the many respectable men, both young and old, who hold women in high esteem and would do anything to help and protect women. Thank you, men of honor.

Sexual and other abuses such as physical, psychological and verbal, hurt to the core, and have lasting effects, even to the point of feelings of unworthiness and brokenness. In the first incident, I was confused, embarrassed and shocked. I did not tell Mama, my aunt, or anyone. If I had told my aunt, it would have been an embarrassing brawl in the yard. He never let me forget it, and he kept taunting me whenever he saw me. I ran to Mama in the second incident, but I did not tell her what happened; maybe because I was afraid again. When the third incident occurred, I ran to Mama and this time I told her what happened. It's hard to explain how the mind works in incidents of shock and trauma. When an innocent and frightened child is placed into the mix, it does not make for a pleasant combination. It's like oil and water.

The internal message I received from these incidents was that I had to fight and protect myself because Mama may not always be there to rescue me. My feelings remained repressed for several years. However, everything came out during my training to become a clinical hypnotherapist. All the students had to go through hypnosis as part of the program. I experienced new freedom in my mind. I am no longer triggered whenever I hear of rape or abusive stories. Prior to hypnosis, it angered me whenever I heard about a child or woman being abused. Whether that abuse is sexual, physical, emotional or other, it does not matter. All abuse leaves scars that only the abused can feel, deep in the soul, and may carry this emotional pain and issues such as trust and trauma for several years after the abuser has moved on.

For many years, I felt I was a victim of circumstances. I buried my emotional pain and never mentioned it to anyone for fear of reprisal and endless embarrassment and disrespect. I continued to work hard in school, never deviating from my goal of receiving a quality education and moving away from the ghetto lifestyle.

Meanwhile, my grandmother continued to provide all of my school supplies, school uniforms and whatever else I needed. Nothing was in abundance. Mama made tremendous sacrifices for me, even to the point of being without, so I could get what I needed. As a child, I often wondered why my mother and aunt would not help me. I realized as an adult that the vision of a better life was not theirs. It was mine, and they could not see through their dark hearts that the dawn of a fresh day was shining on my life. Some people are afraid of changes and would rather remain in the same position because it is comfortable and would produce the same expected outcome year after year. In other words, they knew what to expect.

Risk-taking was another of my ambitious moves. I took risks without thinking about the next move or the consequences. I knew what I wanted, and I went for it. No one told me I would have to sacrifice to achieve what I wanted. Somehow, I knew that we were poor and that there was no other way to succeed unless I took these drastic steps. I always made the first move, and then I got my grandmother to join me in my quest for learning. Whenever I think about what my grandmother has done for me, it gives me goose-bumps and brings tears to my eyes. I love her and I miss her so much. She went to be with the Lord knowing I would be all right.

The questions remain. Where did I get the impetus to be so creative, so focused, and so ambitious to plan my future in such a way to impact my life positively? How did I know that education was the key to my success? How did I know that I had to fight against the odds to get ahead? I tried to encourage my younger sisters to study. Both of them told me they were no "book worms" and went about their business of childhood activities "without a care in the world." I remained serious and focused on getting an education. Why was I being attracted to education and the bright future I envisioned when I was only a child? There can only be one answer. There was a Supreme Being operating in my life in the most significant and intimate manner. It was the same Supreme Being who visited me at nights while I slept and taught me. I know that HE must have been with me in school during the day to know my struggles, to be able to help me at nights. HE came and helped me when I needed him the most. As an adult, HE has proven himself to be God who has guided and protected me all of my life. He is my Jehovah Raah—the Lord who is my Shepherd.

Throughout my travels, God has been with me. I remember when I lived in the Caribbean, my watch broke. I had no way of telling the time to get up in the mornings. The next morning, I heard loud chirping at my window. I was awakened by a bird that did not stop making loud noises while picking on my bedroom window until I got out of bed. I went into the living room to check the time, and it was exactly 6.30. The same time I usually got up. This bird continued to grace my window every morning at the same time for the next two weeks. When I got paid, I bought an electric clock-radio. I set it up with the alarm and went to bed. The next morning, I was awakened by the sound of the alarm from the clock. I never saw or heard the bird again. Throughout my travels, it seems as though someone was always there to take care of my needs.

I have another bird story. When I was living in the Middle East, the work week began on Sundays and ended on Thursdays. Everyone, Muslims and Christians worshipped on Fridays. One of the teachers kept promising to take me to a Pentecostal church, but never kept his promise. After about three weeks of failed promises, I decided to go to church on the internet. At ten o'clock on Friday mornings, I set up the computer and went to church. I listened to the previous Sunday service. To my surprise, I noticed a bird sitting on my window looking at me. I ignored it the first time. But there was something about this bird. It just sat on the window and stared at me. As soon as the service was over, he flew away. These visits continued for the duration of time I spent in the Middle East. Then, on Wednesday evenings at seven o'clock, two visiting birds came and sat on my window and chatted with each other for about fifteen minutes. One twitted then the other twitted. It seemed as though the discussion was very interesting. They twitted and moved around and shook their heads from side to side. They seemed very happy. I had grown accustomed to these visits and looked forward to them every Wednesday. They never came on any other day during the week. Incidentally, our church had services on Wednesday nights.

I have experienced many miracles throughout the years. God always came to me when I needed him the most. HE has graced me with the power to do the things I could not do by myself. I thank God for granting me this grace that enabled me to strive when I did not know what I was doing. I do not know what I have done to deserve these blessings, but I am grateful. The answer to my childhood questions became obvious. God made me in his image, and he cares about me.

A young child deserves to be loved and cared for and be provided with at least the necessities of life—for example, food, clothing, shelter and some form of security, regardless of the circumstances. In the absence of these, a child can grow up to become very insecure while developing various forms of psychoses.

Even though my biological father did not live up to his parental responsibilities, God had placed male mentors as father figures at strategic points in my life. For example, when my grandmother could no longer work to take care of me, Uncle Andy stepped up to the plate, paid my tuition and gave me everything I needed. He helped me through college and even after I left, until I received my first paycheck. When I moved to Mackenzie, I met Mr. Davis, whom we called Grandad. We attended Calvary Temple Assemblies of God Church. He picked me up on Sunday mornings, Wednesday and Friday nights to go to church. I later met his entire family who was just outstanding. They accepted me as one of their own. They embraced me and treated me with love and kindness when I needed it the most. Then there was Sandy. He was a stranger who came to my rescue when I thought my college life was over because I had nowhere to live. He made the sacrifice so I could finish college. This had to be my God at work.

When I peeked through the curtains of the memory on my life, I could see where God has brought me from and where I could have been without Him. I could only thank Him for His saving grace. I thank my teachers and other adults who bravely allowed me to stand on their shoulders and took my hand and led me to the many successes in my life. I can say again, "It takes a village."

Looking back at my childhood and young life, anyone would think it was a very unusual experience that a child could have endured. But it has made me the woman I am today—a woman of integrity and character, who is thoughtful and respectful among the other qualities of a successful woman. All of my experiences were not humiliating. There were good days and more challenging ones, but altogether a worthwhile endeavor. I believe that my God, Jehovah Ezer, is the Lord my Helper. He has kept me safe and led me down this path for a reason. This path was a stepping stone for greater achievements in my life. It not only prepared me for future successes but to deal, realistically, with life's obstacles and challenges.

This brings me to an incident in the hospital. I was very sick in the Intensive Care Unit and hooked up to many machines and monitoring devices. The sun was shining through the unshaded windows. It did not feel as though the air conditioning was working. The heat was intense. I began to sweat profusely. I could not speak or call for help. I just come out of a coma and was still on life support. I also had a tracheotomy and my hands were tethered to the bed rails. It felt as though I were in an inferno with no way out. I began to recite the 23rd Psalm in my mind. A nurse saw me and came over with towels and a change of clothing. While she was mopping up my sweat, a male nurse appeared and said, "Oh, don't treat my sister like this, let's give her a bath!" The nurse stopped and went to get a container with water and shower gel. After the bath and change of clothing, I felt like a new person. My hands were untethered. When they were finished, I tried to say, "Thank you," but no sound came out. Somehow, I knew that they understood. They both smiled and left. The male nurse suddenly disappeared. The female nurse went into the bathroom. The female nurse later brought my medication and looked in on me before she ended her shift that evening. I never saw the male nurse again. I looked for him for days and nights without success. I knew this was my God at work and he sent an angel to help me.

On another occasion, I sat in my hospital bed alone and feeling sorry for myself and wondering if I would get better to resume a normal lifestyle again. As I sat there in my bewilderment, I noticed the cleaner had a long and steady gaze on me. I tried to look away and not return the gaze.

However, I could see from my peripheral view, he had stopped mopping, our eyes met and we both stared at each other. He said to me, "I have a message for you." I did not answer him. I continued to stare as I wondered what does he have to say to me, I don't know him, and who could have given him a message for me? Then he said, "When you are in the valley don't build a hut, keep moving." He then told me about a website where I could read all about my Father's love. I said, "Thank you." My computer was laying on the bed behind me, I turned around to pick it up, when I looked back, he was gone, bucket and everything. I realized that was an angel sent by God. I found the website and I was blessed. Many times, I thought about this statement and the messenger and how God watches over me. I learned not to succumb to negative circumstances but to do something about them. The valley represents my circumstances. The hut represented a temporary solution and a place where I don't want to be. Moving on meant that I should not dwell in a state of depression, but move toward a solution. I have been in many valleys but I learned to persevere with faith, because I know the grace of God will see me through. "God's got my back."

I mentioned these stories to show that God who had started a good work in me was there throughout my journey. He never left me. He promised to be there and He kept his promise. I have been the recipient of many blessings and I will tell all of my stories someday. During my life's journey God laid out those Blessing Stones for me to walk on along this path. Along the way, I found favor, love, and grace from the most unusual places, waiting for me. I have been able to use these nuggets of experiences I have accumulated along this path to enhance my life's journey further. I am forever grateful for my grandmother, Uncle Andy, my teachers and those brave men and women who shared their wisdom, knowledge, and skills with me and allowed me to stand tall on their shoulders to excel in this world.

This may be surprising, but I am even thankful to my aunt and mother for giving me so much trouble and for making my life a "living hell." I believe that if they left me alone, I would have achieved because I had made life goals for myself. However, I might not have been so determined, driven, and focused on achieving my goals. I have forgiven them because it was the right thing to do. Romans 8:31 says "What, then, shall we say to these things? If God is for us, who can be against us? Amen!

When I think about what I have done, I feel very proud of myself, because most children would have given up or not even attempted such a feat. Many times, I thought of running away. But where would I go? My father did not want me to be a part of his life. My mother did not care about my welbeing. I knew that she would set me up to do domestic work. If I went to a friend's or stranger's house, I could not continue my education. I would have to earn my keep somehow. The only person who cared and was willing to make sacrifices for me was my grandmother. So, I stayed and I am glad I rode out that storm. As an adult, I learned to ride out many storms. I learned to think about situations and be patient before I made decisions. I also learned from this experience that when adversity presents itself, I have to make the adjustments to be successful. There are valuable lessons to learn from adversity. My formative education was priceless, and no doubt propelled me out of the ghetto and into a challenging world. My childhood dream came through. Thanks be to God!

For every young person out there, know that you can always dream dreams, but it takes focus, hard work, and ingenuity to make your dreams become a reality. Sometimes it may not be clear to you. There will always be distractions and obstacles. I encourage you to stay the course on a top level and seek friends and adults who are progressive and forward thinking. If you are the smartest in the group, then you are in the wrong place. Those people should not be your friends. Move out and keep moving farther away. You may not have supportive parents or friends, but remember it is your life to live, and you have the responsibility to determine how you live your life. Never seek to blame, but accept responsibility. This is the mark of an authentic hero. Remember to love, forgive, have the right attitude and be grateful for the smallest blessings that God bestows upon you. These are some of the qualities that would open the floodgates for a world of blessings to come into your world.

I heard my grandmother telling her friends, "You cannot take anything with you when you die," and I have heard some of my male students saying "Why should I study or work hard? I may be killed in the streets or even in my apartment building." Or, "My mother or father don't care about me" and "Why should I care about anyone." This is so sad, and this belief is crippling our minds and thought process as a people. This makes us unable to envision ourselves as being talented and capable of monumental accomplishments with hope and faith. It discourages us as a people to be independent beings with no will to succeed. We should strive to leave this world a better place than we found it. While we traverse this exceptional world, we should work hard for ourselves, have hope for a bright future and leave an inheritance so that the next generation would become stronger than we are. My ancestral history of slavery and the fight for freedom, inclusion and equality has taught me this valuable lesson. It's a lesson to be learned by everyone despite our ethnicity, culture or place of birth.

Always remember that everything happens for a reason. This reason may not be clear to you, but always do the best you can with what you have. There may be something bigger and greater waiting for you around the corner. Recognize your Higher Power, because there is no greater love than the love of God - John 3:16 in the Bible says, "For God so loved the world He gave His only begotten son, that whosoever believe, should not perish but have everlasting life." Look around your home, your environment, your world—study other cultures and people, find your passion, find what motivates you and grab life by the horns. Get involved to make this world a better place. All over the world, young people are doing incredible things and leaving a mark in this world. You are here for a reason. The world is waiting for your stamp of approval. Where will you leave your mark? The journey is yours, and your destiny awaits. May God bless you!

My Second Act

Life is a quest. We are all on a journey. We all started this life in the same way - being born naked, not knowing anything or having any knowledge of our own existence. What makes the immediate differences are our parents, our environment and our socio-economic factors. It

is, therefore, our responsibility to find our passion, help someone along the way, be authentic and make positive changes in this world.

Trust in the Lord with all your heart, And lean not on your own understanding. In all your ways acknowledge Him, And He will direct your paths.

Proverbs 3:5-6

I have been blessed to teach and live in many countries and cultures including North and South America, the Caribbean and the Middle East. I am now on my second act in private practice and hope to continue my work with The American Center for Self- Development, which I have founded. It's a place where young people in crisis can get the help they need in terms of counseling, career development, reduce youth recidivism, clinical hypnotherapy and educational resources. I also spend time in community involvement and volunteer work through the Lions Club, Court Appointed Special Advocate (CASA), Grassroots and my church. I also organize work- shops on high school and college requirements. There is so much more that needs to be done to help our young people to be productive and successful citizens.

I have had an exemplary career in Education and I am grateful for the help I received from everyone whose path I was fortunate to have graced and the many "giants" on whose shoulders I have stood and succeeded, in my quest for knowledge and a better life. It appeared every step I took, my God just placed His angels in strategic positions to help me along life's meandering pathways. I was not expected to break the glass ceiling and reach beyond the clouds for the stars in the skies above. God saw the best in me and He sent help throughout my journey. Sandy always said, "I am God's own child." This makes me feel good inside. I know that God loves and accepts me the way I am.

Along the way, there were mishaps. But I refuse to live the rest of my life in regrets of what my life might have been. My steps were ordered by the Lord. Everyone goes through life changes. How we choose to live is up to us. In retrospect, I could have done some things differently and made other unique choices. But I AM THANKFUL, GRATEFUL, BLESSED and at PEACE with my accomplishments and the life I lived. It is my passion to give back, to help young people in the same way that blessings were freely bestowed upon me. I am using my books as a valuable tool to motivate youths to strive towards making this world a better place.

TRIUMPHS OF A LITTLE GIRL

WORKBOOK

There is a workbook that accompanies this memoir (*Triumphs of a Little Girl Workbook*). It teaches the reader about life and learning. It provides the tools to help you make crucial decisions. It's a step-by-step guide to help with the methods of successful planning of projects, whether one is in elementary, high school, college or in the work environment, and so much more. It culminates with the reader being able to construct a revolutionary new form of a vision board called the Benjamin Project Board for Success. The topics include:

Section 1
Learning from Others
Answering questions from Triumphs of a Little Girl

Section 2
In Search of My Passion   Having a discussion with my younger self

Section 3
Inspirational Quotes - Quotes to keep you inspired
each day "I AM" Encouraging Statements
Gratitude and Appreciation List

Section 4
Creative Visualization
Prayer & Meditation

Section 5
Planning Activities & Scheduling

Section 6
Goal Setting
How to Plan Effectively to Achieve Success

Section 7
Problem Solving
Using the Benjamin Model for Success
6W + H = D + S

Section 8
Brainstorming & Project Mapping
Using the Benjamin Model for Success
6W + H = D + S

Section 9
Constructing The Benjamin Project Board for Success

Thank you for purchasing this book

The purchase of this book will help me to work with youths in foster care, group homes and in the Juvenile Court system. I would like to distribute the Memoir and Workbook free of charge and encourage the youths to work through their issues. I am sure you will agree that our youths are our most valuable asset. Helping them to graduate from high school and college and be passionate to work towards finding viable careers that would motivate them to make a valuable contribution to our society.

CPSIA information can be obtained
at www.ICGtesting.com
Printed in the USA
LVHW051733090723
751812LV00013B/786